THE LINK TO SENIOR GOLF:

HOW TO PLAY BETTER AND

HAVE MORE FUN

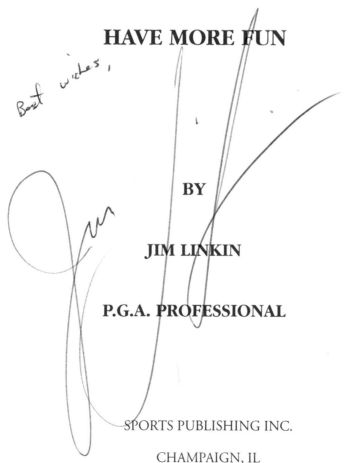

BY

JIM LINKIN

P.G.A. PROFESSIONAL

SPORTS PUBLISHING INC.

CHAMPAIGN, IL

Editor, book design: Susan M. McKinney
Book layout: Lisa J. Peretz
Cover design: Julie L. Denzer

ISBN:1-57167-241-9
Library of Congress Catalog Card Number: 98-85665

Printed in the United States

SPORTS PUBLISHING INC.
http://www.SportsPublishing.com

To my wife Debbie, your love inspires me.

To my parents, for taking the time to teach me.

To our families, for your endless encouragement.

To my students, your passion to learn brings great joy to my life.

To God, thank you for it all.

C O N T E N T S

As a P.G.A. professional and golf school owner, I have been blessed with the honor of spending my days helping others learn to play the game that I have such passion for. Through all my time teaching, I have observed a pattern develop with golfers as they approach their senior years. Their flexibility and strength level begin to change, then they often struggle to perform a swing that no longer fits their body. That's where my experience comes in, and I truly enjoy sharing it with others. As you will see, there are some basic changes that need to be made, both mental and physical, that can change your game and make golf more fun than it's ever been. That is what this book is about; a reflection of the patterns that I have seen on the lesson tee over the years. I will explain the reasons that we need to make adjustments in our minds and bodies, and give you an easy way to accomplish both through thoughts and drills. We will discuss flexibility and how to increase yours. You will understand how today's equipment can help you, and what clubs should not be in your bag. There are instructions for a basic swing motion that we all should have, and how we can fit it to our own bodies. You will learn the importance of the short game, pitching, chipping, putting, and bunker play, and methods to become razor-sharp at all of them. Can you play and practice more effectively? The answer is yes, when you utilize tricks like the Bifocal Backswing and the D.W.I.T. course management system described in this book. It will not only enlighten you on the latest teaching methods, but will provide lots of fun doing so. Ladies, there is a special section for you to address a few additional things you should know about your swing that don't apply to the men.

Wait a minute! How can one swing work for everyone? Simply put, it can't. What we need to do is build a foundation around a few basic principles, and let your body dictate what style you will use. There are almost 25 million golfers in the United States, and nearly half are over 40 years of age. I do not believe that over 11 million golfers can swing the same swing. There are too many variables with height, flexibility, strength, and athletic ability to give everyone the same swing. However, if we subscribe to some solid fundamentals specifically tailored to the senior golfer, we can all play better.

My teaching philosophy is reflected throughout this book. It can be summed up as 1)Attitude is everything, 2)Each of us is an individual, so what one person can do may not be possible for the next person, and 3)If the basic functions of a swing work, it's up to the individual to develop style according to their body's capabilities.

I like setting a foundation for all of my students to expand upon. This will prevent the search for the magic cure when something goes off in your swing. There is nothing worse than changing something every week in your golf swing. You feel lost. This book will give you the direction to take to play better and have more fun.

Enjoy your journey through this book. The chapters are written in a way that will allow you easily to refer back to a certain topic for future reference. I recommend that you start by reading the entire book. There are tricks of the trade and solutions to questions that you may have throughout each chapter, and I wouldn't want you to miss a thing. Feel free to make marks at the areas that you need the most help or interest you the most. Then you can go back later and put the principles into practice. Enjoy!

Being Open to Change

D id you ever wonder why we play golf? I have pondered that question many times in my career. Surely during our worst rounds we ask ourselves what we are doing on the course, but somehow we always return, seeking the better round we know is inside us. The perfect tee shot, a chip that stops inches from the hole, a long putt that falls, these all give us a sense of accomplishment, yet those are only moments in a much bigger picture. So why do we play? The answer is different for everyone, I suppose. Some of the reasons we play are fun, the camaraderie, exercise, and the challenge golf offers. Since it is such a difficult sport to master, there is a respect that comes with playing well. Everyone loves to watch a good player strike the ball, that effortless swish of the club, the click at impact, and the resulting distance that boggles the mind. It is not unlike ballet, a performing art that is enjoyed by not only the one doing it, but also those who choose to watch. During a game of golf, we can go on vacation from our everyday lives for a few hours and be in a beautiful place filled with greenery and wildlife. We can enjoy the company of others, yet stand on the first tee while others watch and feel very alone. Golf gives and takes, but can never be conquered. A golf course can have many different personalities, sometimes simple, sometimes complex, but always a challenge.

Golf is a game played both physically and mentally, and will test both admirably. There are subtle complexities we become more aware of as we grow and become better players, yet golf can still mystify even the world's best players.

One thing is for sure—the amount of enjoyment we derive from golf is directly proportional to how we play. When we are playing our best, we are generally proud of our accomplishment, and feel good about it. That's not to say when we are not playing our best we are not having fun, it is just more fun to play well.

Confidence and feel are the foundation to playing well. Confidence is the mental state that we all desire when we play, and feel is the translation of our thoughts into action on the course. My belief is that anyone can play better if they want to, it only takes education and practice. It is the education that we will address in this book. The practice is up to you, but we will even give you ways to practice that are fun so you practice more.

We all desire to become better at the game, but the players who take action see their desires become reality. As we travel the road to becoming senior golfers, our bodies and minds continue to change, as they have our whole lives. We are not going to stop the natural progression of time. However, if we are smart, we will make the adjustments necessary with our bodies and minds to play the best golf of our lives. We can also have a good time learning while we change.

This chapter is an overview on some of the changes that we need to make mentally and physically to prepare ourselves for the better golf that lies ahead. If we can tap into the positive aspects of our maturation and reject the negative, you will see how much better our golf can become.

PHYSICAL CHANGES

First we will talk about the physical part of the golf swing. This is the place where we first notice the changes in our body, with strength itself diminishing as we age. In my teaching, I always focus on the positive, and love it when students surpass what they thought their limitations were. Time and time again, senior golfers will come to me bemoaning the fact that they are not as strong as they once were, so they can't hit the ball as far. After they make the proper adjustments in their swing, or achieve a better swing motion that fits their body, they often can play far better than they ever did. They soon realize how little muscular strength means to a good, fundamentally sound swing motion. The golf swing is a motion much like dancing. Does that mean that as you lose strength you can no longer enjoy dancing? Of course not. What you do is rely more on style and knowledge, not athletic ability. How else can you explain the fact that many tour players are just hitting their stride in their mid-forties?

Take a look at the senior tours. These golfers are not skipping a beat after 50, with many of them playing the best golf of their lives. I share this observation with many of my students; I'm better than I was two years ago, and I'm not as good as I will be two years from now. As you will see, if you get smarter, you have no choice but to get better.

It is almost easier if you take up golf later in life. Then you don't compare yourself with your athletic ability when you were in your twenties. Golfers who start later in life have no expectations on how they should play, they just do it and enjoy. If you started golfing when you were a kid, it is harder to put things in perspective. All you can remember is hitting it a mile. You tend to compare your performance now with your performance when you were physically much different. Isn't it funny how you don't remember those wild shots that also went a mile into trouble?

So we have two choices. Our first choice is to put things in perspective and develop a style to offset the loss of raw power in our swings. The second choice is to refuse to change, complain about not being as strong as we once were, and spend the rest of our golfing lives in frustration trying to perform in a way our bodies will not allow.

Do you want to know why I am a better golfer now than I was when I was much stronger? I took choice number 1. I may not have the blasting power that I once had, but I hit it on the center of the club face, hit it straighter, and use what power I have very efficiently to hit the golf ball. In addition to efficiency of motion, I have style. That style continues to develop and change with my body. If I tried to hit it the same way I did 15 years ago, I would have to call 911 after the first swing.

This point was driven home to me a few years ago when my wife and I were visiting family out west. While in a resort town that has an ice skating rink open all year, we stopped for lunch. We were having lunch overlooking the ice and watching the skaters, many of whom were professionals practicing for an upcoming show. They were all in their twenties, very athletic and explosive with the physical power they possessed. After a while, they got tired and took a break. Out onto the ice came a very stylish woman in her late fifties. Her skating caught my eye and everyone around me. She had style and moved beautifully across the ice. She was confident and elegant at the same time. Although she did not attempt any triple aerial maneuvers, she stole the show. What a wonderful sight, this woman who was not as strong as the others, making the best of what she had, and loving life at the same time. Efficiency of motion had taken over where sheer strength once was. Something told me she never considers her strength level when it comes to living life to the fullest. She let style take over, much to the delight of the crowd.

I learned a good lesson that day. Let's look at positive versus negative in all of the physical departments, starting with strength level. If we look at it negatively, we can say we are not as strong as we once were, therefore we cannot play as well as we once did. That, by the way, is a great excuse if you are chopping it around the course. Since the golf swing is not entirely based on power, that really is an excuse for not changing, learning new techniques, getting better at your short game, and gaining style. Simply put, if you want to get better, you must change. If you are unwilling to change, prepare to be stuck in a cycle of excuses and disappointments. That doesn't sound like too much fun to me, I would rather have style.

Now let's take that negative and turn it into a positive. You may not be as strong as you once were, but that can only help you. Now you can learn proper technique without it being ruined by blind strength taking over and wrecking your swing. You will be able to swing to a follow through without landing on your rear. You will be able to feel the club head. You will be gripping the club like a human being, not a vise trying to prevent the club from flying farther than the ball as you try to kill it. You will not pull muscles in your back trying to launch it farther than the space shuttle. Since you can feel the club head, you will be able to release the club, get it closed at impact and stop slicing, rather than the tight-handed, grip and rip, cut across at breakneck speed, open face, hard right rudder slice you may have possessed from time to time. Can all this come as a result of not being as strong as we once were? You bet! As you will learn, we will rely on both levers of the golf swing for power. When we swing hard with muscle power, it actually prevents the second lever from working well unless you have tremendous experience and even then nothing is guaranteed. That is why when you see a professional swing it looks so effortless. It is!

Here is another negative. "I can't go back as far, because I'm not as flexible as I was a while back." What a shame, the lack of elasticity to your muscles won't let you go back to beyond parallel in the back swing. Now we will get right in to the good news. The senior swing described in this book is more compact than anything you have ever tried. You do not have to take the club anywhere past where you feel comfortable on the back swing. You will never have to force a back swing again. As you will see, once you get past your comfort level on the back swing, disaster strikes. We will also learn ways to become more flexible through stretching. We will learn to warm up correctly to prevent pulled muscles, sore body parts, and bad shots. Again, by warming up various students every day, I feel more flexible now than I did years ago. You will too.

What about arthritis and other physical limitations? If you suffer from arthritis, they now make grips that are large and extra coarse to help the arthritic hand get a better grip. Shaft technology has offered up some lightweight graphite shafts that will make some of the clubs you may have used in the past feel like sledgehammers. Golf balls that are specifically designed to get the most out of whatever swing speed you generate are available by many companies.

I feel the most significant changes have come in the golf swing itself. Things that were taught twenty years ago have been up dated and are much easier to comprehend and perform. With these updates, teaching golf has become more simple than ever. We will discuss more on the mechanics of the swing in the following chapters, first we need to talk about the mental side of golf and how we need to adjust our attitude equally as we adjust our swing. As with our swing, we should not be expected to think the same way as we did years ago, we should think better.

ATTITUDE

I wish everyone could spend a day in my shoes as a P.G.A. professional and instructor to realize how big a role attitude plays in your golf game. That should come as no surprise. By now we should have all figured out that attitude has a lot to do not only with our performance in golf, but also our performance in life. You are the only one in charge of your attitude. Remember this–if you think you are going to fail, you will. If you think you cannot learn, you won't. Conversely, if you have a will to succeed, you will. If you want to learn, no one can stop you. If you desire to get better, you must.

I feel fortunate that the students who come to see me do so because they want to improve. No one is forcing them to seek help with their game, they come of their own free will. That leads to a lot of people with good attitudes. Not many people want to spend money to learn something and then have a bad attitude ruin their chances at success.

An important facet of my job is to offer encouragement to others. If you were to ask me what I think I am on this earth for, I would say it is to encourage others. Now before you start thinking that is easy coming from some spoiled kid who grew up at a country club, think again. I did grow up at a club, but as a caddie, not a member. I lugged bags and earned every round I was able to play on caddie day. I then played public courses my whole life. I really only got to play at clubs after I was hired as one of their assistant professionals. I have overcome severe vision problems and couldn't care less, because some people can't see at all and I feel thankful that I can. So when I say you can do it, it comes from my heart.

Attitude plays such an important role that it can sometimes overcome obstacles that seem too big to conquer. I have been blessed with the responsibility and honor of teaching thousands of people to golf in my career. I respect each and every one for trying to learn something new instead of plowing through a life with no new challenge. I would have to say the greatest tool any golfer can take with him or her is a positive attitude. With a good attitude, a problem in your swing becomes a temporary setback, not the end of the world. With the right attitude, a bad hole becomes a challenge to fight back from, not a signal to quit and stop caring. You will be able to learn more quickly instead of beating up on yourself and not getting anywhere. You will be able to handle disappointment better too. I remember reading something a long time ago that did not make much sense at the time, but became more clear as time went on. It was about how difficult golf is and stated that you must learn to lose in golf before you can learn how to win. You will lose much more often than you win. A good attitude can help handle this low winning percentage, and let you savor the times that you come out on top.

Golf is about overcoming obstacles, small and large. Whether it's the bad bounce off the cart path and out of bounds, or a surgery that almost ends your career, we all have things to overcome. Our attitude will help us or hurt us. A good attitude can also help us put things into perspective. It is very difficult not to be selfish with our own problems, yet when we look at others' troubles, ours don't look so big.

I'll share a little story on attitude. Everyone who knows me remarks on my positive attitude and the fact that I am a very happy person. I have no reason not to be happy, for I am blessed with a wonderful life. I do suppose, though, that if I were somewhere else doing something different, that I would still be as happy. That is a choice that I make every morning when I wake up. I make my own attitude and you should, too.

In my career I have been fortunate enough to teach golf to people who are physically challenged. Auto accident victims, boat crashes, blind golfers, you name it and I have had the chance to instruct them. We can learn from each and every one of these people; not just about their golf swings, but their attitudes.

I'll share the journey of one such man. I met him a few years back and his attitude changed my life. His name is Marcel Laniel. One day this man called on the phone at the club I was working at and said he was recommended to me by someone to take some golf lessons. He explained that he had some sort of problem, and I asked him to come on down, there's nothing I can't fix. When he got there, I couldn't believe my eyes. His lovely wife Andrea came to the shop first and said her husband was following her.

Down the path came Marcel, not able to walk more than an inch or two at a time. He had recently recovered from a massive stroke that had paralyzed his left side. Only his right side worked and he kind of dragged the left side. Here was a determined man. I was astounded by his resolution to make it to the shop unassisted.

We sat on the bench and talked. He had been a golfer for a long time before the stroke. His wife talked of the endless hours he looked out the window, longing for another chance to hit a ball. I did not know what to say except that we would try. I could see from the start that Marcel wanted no special treatment because of his disability. He wanted no sympathy either, he was thankful to be alive and out of the apartment.

I learned how to hit with one hand so I could instruct him better. He would balance on his right foot and use his left foot as an outrigger so he did not fall. We started slowly, but I worked him hard, and he practiced hard. There were plenty of times he lost his balance and stumbled, but he never once complained. His attitude and faith kept him going. Through it all, we had an ongoing joke. He would smile and say, "The doctor told me I would never walk again, but he didn't say anything about golf."

By the end of the season, we were playing nine holes and Marcel was a new man, as was I. It did not matter how far he hit the ball, he was outside in a beautiful place with his wife and friends doing something that he never thought he would do again. We became very good friends and still stay in touch. Without his wife, his attitude, his faith and his courage, he would still be sitting looking out the window, or worse. Thanks Marcel, for teaching me about attitude so that I may teach others.

GETTING SMARTER WITH TIME

Golf is a thinking person's game. The more clearly we can reason, the better chance we have of making good on-course decisions. We need to start using our experience to our advantage, instead of focusing on what our bodies can or cannot do. Our knowledge is an area that we can tap into that we have more of than in the past. Call it wisdom or smarts, call it anything you like. The fact is, as we get older, we have more experiences to draw from, and we are able to reason more clearly. I guess that is why my Dad will always be smarter than I am. He always seems to have good advice, and he should, he has more experience. I am not afraid to seek the advice of those whom I feel have more wisdom than I do. That is one of the ways we learn.

You may wonder how you can apply this to golf. We can learn about the game from those who know more than we do. We can also retain more. The chances of making dumb mistakes on the golf course more than once greatly diminish as we mature. I don't know about you, but I surely am getting smarter with age. We need to use this ability to think things out rationally to our advantage, both on the golf course and as we practice. We must practice wisely, not just hammer balls. We can think our way around the course more clearly. We can also learn from our past experiences better.

Think of another positive and time management comes to mind. Many of us will have more time on our hands as we retire. Now is the perfect time to become as good as you always wanted to be. We can practice and play more. If we practice effectively, we have the time and patience to learn the right way to hit a ball. You will have time to devote to your short game, which is something that you probably have not done in the past. Think of how you could score if you could get up and down from anywhere. If we have more time on our hands, we will also be able to get fitted for equipment that suits our swing, and try it out before we buy it. Proper equipment and custom fitting are vital to the senior swing and are discussed in detail in chapter three. So as we become more free with our time, let's devote some time to getting better at our game. The more you put in, the more you will get back. I can't think of a better time to be the golfer you always wanted to be.

TO SUM IT UP

To summarize, we know that our bodies are changing, as are our strength level and flexibility. If we look at these changes as negatives, we are not going to reap the many benefits that golf has to offer. We must look at these changes in a positive light. Know that we are smarter than we once were. Know that the patient, relaxed golfer who is playing her best will always enjoy the game more than the golfer who storms around berating herself for how bad she is.

Most importantly, remember that attitude is the most significant of all the changes that we must make. If we maintain a good attitude, we will have the golfer's greatest weapon in our arsenal—patience—and the ability to enjoy the greatest game of all.

CHAPTER 2

Getting Your Body Ready to Play

There are many things besides the mechanical swing motion that can affect our golf game. In this chapter we will look into these things and try to stack the deck in our favor before we ever tee the first ball up in a round. We will explore the different body styles and how they will affect your choice of swing keys. You will learn some swing killers, things that can ruin your game before you go to the course. Also, there are numerous exercises you can do to add flexibility to your body and warm yourself up correctly at the golf course before you play.

These are areas that are important, whether you are already a senior golfer, or on your way to becoming one. We will get started first by looking at different body styles and seeing how they affect your swing.

WE ARE ALL DIFFERENT

The first thing you realize when you set your sights on becoming an instructor of golf is that there are many different types of people playing the game, and they come in all shapes and sizes. As teachers, we all have certain principles that we feel are important and we focus on.

That is how instructors develop their own style. Professionals must be careful to take into consideration differences in golfers' bodies, swing style, flexibility and strength level when they are teaching. The most common complaint I hear from senior students is that they tried to learn something their body would not accept. This can certainly be a blow to your confidence.

You feel like you are stupid because you can't grasp a particular concept, when in fact it's a simple error of not matching the swing to the swinger. I hate to see people struggle; it is my nature to be concerned about my fellow golfers. I believe much of the struggle is self-imposed, because golfers ask their bodies to do the impossible. You know your body better than anyone else, so you must make the call. If I tried to swing like the new stable of 20-year-old superstars, it would sound like someone stepping on twigs—you could pick up my pieces and roll me home in a wheelbarrow. Does that mean I still can't play a good game of golf? Of course not; I just can't swing as I did when I was in my twenties. I could try, but chances are I would be disappointed. I am in my forties, and there are easier, more efficient ways to accomplish the same results.

We must keep in mind that different bodies dictate different swing styles. They are not etched in stone, but the majority of these body styles have certain characteristics that are common to that style. As we go through these body styles, try to find the one that fits as close to yours as possible. This will give you insight into what your swing tendencies are.

Remember, no golfer will have an advantage or be better because of how he is built. It is the one who puts his build to the best use who will do the best. We will start with height. Let's take three different golfers, all with different heights. Even though they are all performing the same basic movements, their swings will take slightly different paths due to how they stand over the ball at address.

The tall golfer will stand more erect and have a more upright swing. The medium-height golfer will have a less upright swing and stand less erect. The shorter golfer will bend over more and have a slightly flatter swing that goes more around his back. This is a natural set up for all three golfers.

I heard the following explanation once, and liked it. The swing of a taller golfer will follow a path more like a Ferris wheel (up and down), whereas the shorter golfer's swing will follow a path more like a merry-go-round (around). That is no big deal until you start to fight it.

When you start fighting your body's natural tendency, you will start to run into trouble. If the golfers switched set-up positions and tried to play, they would all struggle to maintain their balance during the swing. Take a tall golfer and bend him over too much, and you have a golfer severely out of balance. Take the shorter golfer and stand her upright, and the swing is equally difficult to perform.

Neither golfer can play effectively from these positions. The middle-height golfer is the one with the most leeway and can play from either position as long as it is not too severe. The bottom line is that all of these golfers must be balanced for their body styles. As you may have guessed by now, the way each golfer's equipment fits him or her is going to have a bearing on the set up. We will go over club fitting in the equipment chapter, and give you an education on what makes a golf club good for you.

Your build has something to do with your swing and set up, too. If you are slightly built, you can generally stand taller or more upright as opposed to a person who is more stocky and needs to bend over a little more. The more stocky golfer will have his hands slightly farther away from his body. He also will swing more around (merry go round) than up (Ferris wheel).

Can your strength level have any bearing on your swing? Most definitely. If you are a strong person, you probably will have a slightly shorter swing than a person who is not as strong. A golfer with less upper-body strength will rely on swinging the weight of the club much more. If you have strong wrists and forearms, you will be able to use those parts to your advantage when you swing with a strong release of the wrists at impact.

This brings us to a final point on creating a swing style that fits you; how your own personality fits into your golf swing.

ON TEMPO AND STYLE

Have you ever had anyone who has a long, molasses slow swing tell you to slow down? You try and try, but when you slow down, you hit it worse. Finally after struggling for long enough, you abandoned trying to slow your swing and started hitting it better. You probably struggled because your personality did not match the new swing that you were trying to perform. In all my observations, I see two distinct personalities in golfers' swings. I call them a hit swing, and a swing swing. These swing styles are often a reflection of the golfer's personality.

A hit swing is a shorter, harder, faster swing motion. A swing swing is the long, slow, patient, swing motion. Both are extremely effective if the type of swing fits the golfer and she is not trying to change her natural style. I am a firm believer that this swing personality is a trait of each golfer, and you are born with it. It's like a fingerprint of your golf swing, and is yours alone.

I mention this as a word of caution. I have seen many a golfer struggle in vain trying to change from one style to another. Work with what you were born with, and you will have far more success.

It is also important when we are looking at swing styles to take any injuries into consideration when developing a style. To try to force someone with an injury to swing a certain way is doing that golfer a great injustice. Those with a bad back may have been out of balance their entire golfing careers, thereby aggravating the injury. They would want to get their balance with the weight on the balls of their feet to take stress off the lower back. Certainly shortening their swing and relying on a smooth swing motion would help too.

Golfers with bad knees should stand with their feet slightly open to the target line (left foot flared out and dropped back off the target line a few inches). They can also stand more erect with only a small amount of knee flex. Both of those adjustments will take pressure off the knees. Vision problems and arthritis will be discussed in depth in the following chapters. The bottom line is that we can still play with injuries that have healed as long as the doctor has given us permission and we make the appropriate adjustments.

It is worth noting that those who play after an injury must swing smoothly and listen to their bodies for feedback. Normally your body will tell you if you are overdoing it or not. If you are aggravating an old injury, make the changes needed to stop hurting yourself. Slowing down is a good place to start.

How do you know which style you should be using? First, after taking any injuries into consideration, I would look at the personality of the golfer. Many golfers are type A personalities. They are aggressive and pretty quick at many things that they do. For the most part they wake up early, keep lists, and are often on the go.

Patience may not be a strong point of type A's, so it's really not fair to ask them to fight their personalities for 18 holes and use a long, flowing, slow swing that requires tremendous patience and timing. They will have a very difficult time. Then we have the type B personalities. Normally very content, they like to take their time to do things right. They have patience and can be quite happy relaxing or hanging out. Type B personalities are not known for their aggressiveness; which is reflected in their golf swing. Slow, patient, and often technically beautiful to watch. They are in no big hurry to complete their swing; they are often more patient than type A people in learning the correct swing fundamentals.

What would happen if we asked these types of golfer to speed up their swing? Probably the same bad result as if we asked a hit swinger to slow down too much. The next time you are watching tour players, pick out which golfers have which styles. It is also not a bad idea to find a tour player with a similar build and swing style as you have, and make a mental picture of his swing to copy.

Although I know of no studies that give exact percentages, I know from my own observations that there are many more type A personalities golfing than type B people. I think it is the competitive nature of type A's that makes them want to golf. This is also why I may have a student who is a real golf nut, yet can't get her spouse or friend interested. She can't understand how her friend or husband could not be completely taken by the game, as she is.

Since I am a P.G.A. professional, golf school owner, and instructor, everyone expects that my wife, Debbie, is a certified golf nut. She loves the game, but also has other interests. She is a type B person, and I am a type A. You could wake me up at 2 o'clock in the morning and tell me we were going to play golf with flashlights, and I would ask you when we tee off. Deb would stay home and sleep. She has a long, patient, flowing swing. Mine is short, back and to the point. Each is effective in its own way.

Type A and type B styles and golfers; we know that opposites attract, so look closely. It is always better not to force the game on anyone, as much as you would like them to play. Let their curiosity peak until they ask you. Don't press the issue.

We must also know our tendencies as they relate to our practice. Type A people want immediate results. That is the bad news, as we know in golf there are not many changes we can quickly turn into a comfortable feel. The good news is that type A's are also very determined in their search for results. This can sometimes counteract a lack of patience.

Type B people, when they golf, are very patient, relaxed practicers, that can hit many shots and not be too concerned with the results as long as they see some improvement in feel. I don't worry much about the type B's, it's the type A's who need to pay close attention here.

If you are a type A golfer, make your practice interesting so you do not get bored or complacent. Hit lots of different shots with lots of different clubs. Go with a friend and have a competition like the ones I described in chapter nine. Go with a purpose, not only to hit balls. Take frequent breaks to slow yourself down. It's not that you want to slow your swing down. It is in between swings that we need to slow our pace.

Let's review this section before we go on. We want to develop a style that complements our body style and personality. We should balance properly in accordance to our height, with taller golfers standing taller or more upright and shorter golfers bending over slightly more. If you are thin or slightly built, you too will stand slightly taller. If you have a stocky build, you will bend over more with your hands a little farther from your body.

Match your swing to your personality, too. A hit swing, which is a quicker, shorter, to-the-point kind of swing, is usually what type A personalities use, and rightfully so. The swing swing is a longer, slower flowing swing that suits the type B personalities very nicely. The bottom line is if you are a high-energy, nuclear-powered type A ball of fire, don't waste your time trying to develop a slow, syrup-smooth swing. You will be better off working on the basic fundamentals and learning to keep them intact at a quicker pace. For you type B's, it's just nice to see you out there golfing.

FLEXIBILITY AND STRETCHES

Are you as flexible as you were when you were in your twenties? I don't see a lot of hands up out there, but don't fret; neither am I. By now you have probably noticed that there are different flexibility levels that we reach during our lives. Children seem to be made out of rubber, and can twist in ways that would leave us looking for the heating pad. Teenage golfers are still very flexible, and strong too. It is usually in our thirties and forties that we start to feel less flexible, and we need to start thinking about stretching to regain some range of motion in our bodies. But not everyone is the same, and we all have different levels of flexibility. I think that I have been blessed with stiffness my whole life, so I never became spoiled by what might have been. I know this for sure—if I do not warm up with some stretching before I play, I will not play as well as when I do. That in itself is enough to make me warm up before I go out or practice. I want every advantage I can get.

You cannot imagine how many times students come to me with their scorecards and say "Jim, as you can see I started off poorly, but once I warmed up, I really played great!"

That's when I respectfully ask why they didn't warm up before they went out. A giant light bulb usually rises above their head and they proclaim, "What a great idea!" This will usually be followed with a scorecard the next week, a smile, and a finger pointing out a much better start on the second card. It makes sense. I don't know a professional in the world who gets out of the car, ties on his shoes, jumps up on the tee, and rips it.

Since we don't use our golfing muscles often in everyday life, they are not ready at a moment's notice. As we lose flexibility, they really don't want to cooperate, so it's up to us to warm them up correctly. I don't mean hitting four jumbo buckets before you go out to play, either. I am going to give you two sets of flexibility stretches to do. One is the major package that I do at home, and the other is the final set that I do at the golf course or range to prepare to practice or play. The first set of stretches is the big one to do at home. These will expand your range of motion and make you feel better, not to mention help you hit the ball better. The second group of stretches is for right before you tee off or hit balls at the range.

They only take about two minutes to do, so you can do them even if you are running late to the tee. They are to warm up your muscles so you don't pull any as you are swinging during your round or practice session. You will not be as sore when you come home from playing, either! Before we get into the actual stretches, I have a story that relates to stretching to help make my point.

I do these stretches every single morning without fail. I know I will be hitting demonstration shots during lessons, and I sure don't want to be stiff when I do. I wouldn't think of hitting a ball without warming up. I learned this lesson the hard way about five years ago. I had just gotten to work, when one of my students proudly showed me his new radar-guided, boron-shafted, giant something or other that was guaranteed to hit the ball past Mars or your money back. He was not having any luck with it at all, couldn't even get one off the launch pad, so he asked me to try it for him. Now, as a P.G.A. professional, I pride myself with being able to hit anyone's equipment to show them how it should work. Without thinking, I got up and hit a series of the worst shots I have ever hit in my life, all clunks with no style.

I realized immediately what the problem was, that I had not warmed up correctly, but the damage was already done. I found out later that he sent the driver back for a full refund because not even the professional could hit with it, and did I feel dumb. As I stood in the shop holding my aching back, I vowed never to swing again without warming up correctly. Luckily, we blamed the driver, but I couldn't swing for three days from the pulled muscles in my back.

Let's use these stretches, learn from my mistakes, and warm up properly to give ourselves the best chance of playing well and not getting hurt.

Here is an important rule: BEFORE STARTING ANY STRETCHING OR EXERCISE PROGRAM, GET PERMISSION FROM YOUR DOCTOR. This is important. I don't know you personally, and I don't know what condition you are in. Your doctor does, so ask him for permission.

This first group of stretches and exercises are the ones that you should do at home as often as you can. If you do these every day, you will see your flexibility and strength increase significantly. You do not have to start with all of them at once. As your body accepts them, increase the number of stretches and exercises that you do and increase the repetitions of them as well. Never bounce, jerk hard, or do any of these abruptly. You want to smooth into these positions. Try to get on a schedule at home doing these exercises. I do mine every morning, and I feel like I am shortchanging myself if I can't do them. I always feel good when I am done, and I supplement these with a brisk walk as often as I can. If you can take a short, brisk walk to warm up, it will help. If you can't go outside and walk, you can walk in place first to loosen yourself up, then away you go.

Stretch #1: The cat and dog. Kneel on the floor like I am doing here (Figure 2.1). Make sure that your hands are directly below your shoulders and your knees are directly below your hips. Slowly arch your back and hold it for a few seconds. Then relax it. Do this 10 times very slowly. Your dog or cat may join you, which is fine. This is a good stretch for your lower back.

Figure 2.1. The cat and dog.

Stretch # 2: Knee to the chest. As long as you are down on the floor, we might as well stretch out the lower back some more.

This is an area that seniors need to keep limber and relaxed. While laying on your back, gently pull your right knee up toward your chest (Figure 2.2). You should feel stretching going on in your lower back and buttocks. Don't pull too hard and don't go farther than you can comfortably. Hold that position for several seconds and release it. Now do the same stretch with your left knee. I usually like to hold each knee for about 10 seconds, then I do the other knee. I will repeat each knee several times.

Figure 2.2. The knee to the chest.

Stretch # 3: Both knees to the chest. You are still on the ground, so let's do both knees at the same time (Figure 2.3). Gently pull the knees toward your chest. Feel your lower back stretch. Hold for a few seconds and gently release them. Repeat this one several times too. This is another great stretch for your lower back and legs.

Stretch # 4: The crunch. While you are still on the floor , we can do one more exercise that is good for the stomach and back, the crunch. You can fold your hands across your chest or lace them together behind your neck (Figure 2.4). Flex your knees so they are off the floor like I am doing in the picture. Your back should be flat

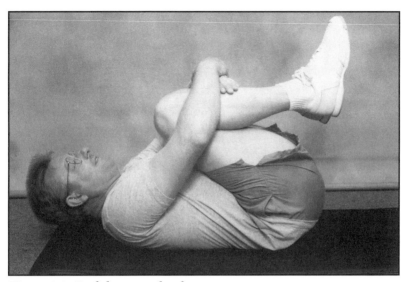

Figure 2.3. Both knees to the chest.

on the floor too. Raise your whole upper body slightly off the floor until your shoulder blades don't touch the floor. This is a great exercise for the stomach muscles and will even build some muscle in the lower back along the way. If you have not done this one before, it's tricky, so don't over do it when you are just starting. Repeat a few times at first. As you get comfortable with your endurance level, you can increase the repetitions and frequency of this one.

Stretch # 5: Push away from the wall. Find a wall that has some open area. Either make sure it's in a spot where it doesn't matter (garage or basement) or make sure your hands are clean so you don't leave fingerprints. I have warned you, so if you get in trouble for messing up the wall, you're on your own. Stand about 18 inches away from the wall and put your hands against the wall fingers pointing up as I am doing in the picture (Figure 2.5). Slowly allow yourself to fall toward the wall, supporting yourself with your hands. No other part of your body should ever touch the wall except your hands. As your face approach the wall, start pushing away slowly in the other direction until you are standing straight up again.

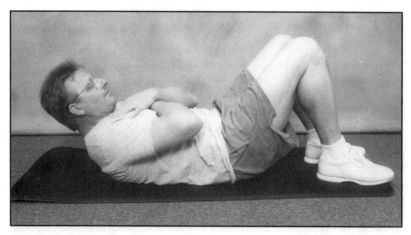

Figure 2.4. The crunch.

Another good spot to do this is the doorway to a room. This is a resistence exercise that will not only stretch you out through extension, but will build muscle in your arms, chest, and shoulders. It is like doing a push up while standing up, which is much more friendly on your body. Repeat this until you feel it in your arms and chest muscles. Again, you want to start off with only a few at the beginning, then increase how many you do as you see fit.

Figure 2.5. Push away from the wall.

Stretch # 6: Hamstring on the stairs. Find a stair with a railing. Stand erect and while holding the railing for balance, lift one leg onto the first stair as I am doing in the picture (Figure 2.6). Gently press down until you feel the muscle on the inside of your thigh stretch. The first time you do this stretch, you will realize just how inflexible your legs may have gotten. When I started doing these exercises, I could hardly lift my leg to the first stair without it hurting as it stretched. Now I can raise my leg to waist height without a problem, and use my legs in the golf swing much more effectively. When you get done with the first leg, do the same thing with the other leg. As the days go by, you will begin to raise the height that you put your leg to start, but at the beginning, start low. Repeat a few times.

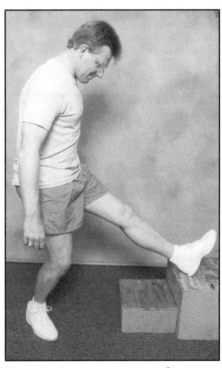

Figure 2.6. Hamstring stretch.

Stretch # 7: Trunk rotation. Standing tall, put your hands on your head. Slowly rotate in a circular motion from one side to the other(Figure 2.7). Go very slowly. This is a super stretch for the muscles in your back. As you loosen up, you can start to speed up your turns slightly, and get a good rhythm going. Repeat as many times as you like.

Stretch # 8: Lat muscle stretch. With your hands on top of your head, lightly stretch side to side (Figure 2.8). Start very slowly and only go a little at a time. You will feel these muscles stretching almost immediately. These are the same muscles that many golfers pull when they swing too hard without warming up. Take my word on this one, as I speak from experience. I pulled these muscles early in my career when I didn't realize the value of stretching before you rip it off the tee. For one week I couldn't even breathe without them

Figure 2.7. Trunk rotation.

hurting. Hopefully, this stretch will prevent you from going through the same thing. These are very much like the hamstrings, muscles that most people never knew they had, never mind stretched. So take it easy at first, only stretch in small increments and don't rush. Repeat a few times at first. Make it part of your daily stretches.

Figure 2.8. Lat muscle stretch.

Stretch # 9: Tippy toes. Hold a countertop for balance and simply go from flat footed to your toes and back down flat footed again (Figure 2.9). You can do this one as you are brushing your teeth. Great for the legs, ankles, and buttocks. Go slowly and repeat as many times as you want. This is one of the easiest ones, and fun, too.

Stretch # 10: Slow motion golf swings. Hold your left thumb with your right hand and do slow motion golf swings like I am doing in the pictures (Figures 2.10.1 and 2.10.2). Start from over an imaginary ball, slowly do your back swing, and go to a full finish and hold your follow through.

This is a good drill to do when you want to work on your swing, but don't

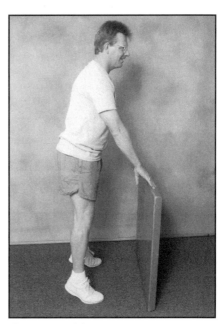

Figure 2.9. Tippy toes.

have a club in your hand. Notice this stretch is last. You must make sure the rest of the muscle groups are warmed up before you swing, whether you have a club in your hand or not. I always start off very slowly and slightly increase the speed as I go along. Make sure you have enough room to swing. By the way, don't worry if your follow through isn't too good at this point, we will fix it in chapter four. Do this one 10 times to start, and then increase it to how ever many you feel comfortable with.

Figure 2.10.1 Slow motion golf swing.

These stretches are designed to help your range of motion and flexibility. How often should you do them? Every day if you can. These are not strenuous exercises like weightlifting. They are to be done softly, not abruptly. You should feel better and looser after doing these, not ready to take a snooze. How many of each exercise should you start with? It depends on your level of fitness and what your doctor says. If you don't do any stretching now, one of each exercise is one more than you did yesterday. Increase your repetitions each day until you are at a comfortable number of each and you feel limber. For some golfers, that means 25 of each, for others it means 10. It is best to get a program you feel good with, and stick to it. Stretching will pay great dividends on the golf course and off, in the way you play and feel.

Figure 2.10.2 Slow motion golf swing.

Those are what I call our at home stretches. These will keep our muscles in a more limber state to do whatever we come up against in our day-to-day lives, whether we are golfing, gardening, or just working around the house. But how about when we get to the course? Are our muscles ready for what we are about to ask them to do? The answer is no. If we take two minutes to do our at the course stretches, we will be more ready to swing, and in turn will give ourselves another opportunity to play better. Here is why. The rotary back motion that is required for the golf swing is not a motion we do often during a normal day, unless of course you do what I do for a profession. Even if we have done our at home stretches, they were at home, not at the course. Our muscles may also be stiff from riding in the car to the course. If we are warmed up correctly, we can hit our first tee shot as if we have played a few holes.

Since the first shot will also set some of your mental tone for the game, don't you want to give yourself the best chance to hit it well? Lastly, we might be running late for our tee time. If you only have five minutes to warm up before teeing off, it is better to spend it stretching and then hitting a few putts rather than rushing to the range and trying to hit some balls at lightning speed. Stretching is a much better use of your time. Remember, again, to check with your doctor before you do these or any other exercises.

Here is the exact routine I do before teeing off. It has worked wonderfully for me and will work for you, too. It warms you up, yet won't wear you out.

Warm up # 1. Take any long iron and put it behind your neck as I have done in the picture (Figure 2.11). If behind your neck is beyond your range of motion, then holding it across your chest will work quite well also. Get into your golfing posture by bending a little at the waist. Add a small amount of knee flex. Slowly rotate as far around as you can until you feel resistance, then go the other way. Do this forty times.

Figure 2.11. Warm up #1: Put a long iron behind your neck and gently rotate around from one side to the other.

Warm up # 2: Find a stair or you can use the back of the golf cart. Hold onto something so you don't fall. If you can't find anything to hold onto, Turn two clubs over and use them as canes for balance as I am doing in the picture (Figure 2.12). Raise your foot up onto the stair and stretch the muscles in your legs slowly. Do both legs for about 20 seconds each.

Warm up # 3: Slowly reach down and bend as you are trying to touch your toes (anywhere near your toes is actually fine). Contrary to popular belief, you do not have to keep your legs rigid as you do this stretch, extended is fine. Go slowly, no jerking, no bouncing. Do this four times.

Figure 2.12. Warm-up #2: It's always smart to stretch the muscles in your legs before you swing.

Warm up # 4: Hold a club by the ends with both hands directly above your head. Slowly stretch by bending to one side and holding it for a few seconds. Then slowly go to the other side and do the same thing, no bouncing, no jerking and don't force it farther than you are comfortable with. As you have probably noticed, this is very similar to the lat stretch that is part of our daily exercise and stretching program, only we are holding our golf club. Do this stretch four times.

Now you are warmed up enough to at least start taking some practice swings. My first practice swings are always very easy and slow. Smoothness counts, and I gradually increase the speed until I am taking full swings at my regular swing speed. This will take you all of about three minutes, and as you will see, it is the best three minutes you can invest into your game when you are on the way to the first tee. If after you do your warm-up stretches you still have a minute or two, go to the putting green. Since so many of the strokes you will put on the score card are putts, it is a worthwhile investment in time. If it gives you a better feel for the greens, then I'm all for it.

Do you get a chance to walk the course once in a while? If you do, that is great. Walking can do wonders for the soul, not to mention the cardiovascular system. If you can't walk the course, any walk is good for you, even if it's around your neighborhood.

SWING KILLERS THAT AFFECT SENIORS

There are three things that senior golfers need to be aware of that I call swing killers. They are stress, exhaustion, and dehydration. In my experience in teaching and playing with many different golfers, these three conditions cause many bad rounds, and should be avoided. Let's take them one at a time.

By the time you have reached your mid-forties, you have either been able to reduce the stress in your life considerably, or you have learned to deal with it. But there are times when stress pops back up and rears its ugly head. If you are in a particularly stressful time of your life, or have a stressful situation that you are going through, you need to lower your expectations if you go golfing. Golf is a sport that requires significant concentration for short periods of time.

When you are stressed out, it is very difficult to concentrate at all. If you have stress in your life and still want to go golfing, expect nothing and remember why you are there, for fun and exercise. You are there to try to reduce the stress you are under. You do not want to increase your stress level by getting upset at your inability to concentrate or shoot a good score. Just relax, lower your expectations, and take a nice walk in the park. We will discuss performance pressure that we feel on the course in a later chapter. A solid pre-shot routine will make us forget the pressure and change our focus to the task at hand. We need to lower our expectations anyway if we are under stress, so we can use golf as the great escape it should be.

Time pressure also puts you under loads of stress. One of the worst things you can do to yourself is say, "I only have an hour, I'm going to try to play as many as I can." I think that you would be better off practicing your putting or chipping. If you do want to go out on the course, shoot for quality, not quantity. It would be better to play three good holes where you did a good pre-shot routine, picked the right clubs, and played well rather than rush around nine holes and hit it sideways. This situation presents itself on the driving range too. You only have 15 minutes, yet you are trying to set the world record for balls hit in that amount of time. If you are going to be rushed, which can happen, putt instead. At least you can develop some feel on the putting green in a short amount of time. Slow yourself down and make that time count.

Exhaustion is the second swing killer for seniors. You need to be well rested to play golf. If you are tired, you not only can't think as well as normal, but your body will not react to what you want it to do. Obviously if you know you are playing the next day, get a good night's sleep. If you are very tired, maybe skip the game and practice a little instead. If you absolutely, positively must play and you are tired, lower your expectations again. You will not be able to play your best, so don't expect to. A funny thing about lowering your expectations; sometimes when you do, you play very well because you are relaxed and not expecting too much.

Another swing killer is dehydration. I went to a seminar by one of the major sports drink manufacturers and could not believe how much water it takes to stay hydrated when you are golfing. It really does not have to be hot out for you to lose moisture from your body when you are out on the golf course. Seniors are particularly prone to dehydration. Here is the key, you want to start drinking fluids well before you start dehydrating. Drink one 16-ounce bottle of sports drink (Gatorade, Powerade, etc.) or water before you get to the course, and then drink lots of water or sports drink during your round. Since some of those drinks taste pretty strong to me, I mix half water, half sports drink and it tastes good. I make sure I drink water at every cooler along the way. When you live in Florida, you learn to force liquids in, even if you don't think you are thirsty. You don't have to bloat yourself, but you should be replacing fluids all the way around the course.

I know what it feels like to get dehydrated and it is not pretty. I was playing a 36-hole qualifier in Orlando, Florida a few years back. It was September, and if you know anything about Orlando in September, it can get kind of hot and humid. The professionals down there are smart. They don't get little cans of sport drinks, they all take half-gallon jugs of the stuff with them in summer tournaments. Those are the days that your shirt has white salt stains all over it by the fourth hole! Anyway, I played 27 holes at a couple over par and I was feeling good. I had run out of drink on the front nine of the second round, but I wasn't worried, I had drunk a half gallon. On about the 15th hole my legs started to get wobbly and I got a little light headed. Shortly thereafter, I lost control of what my muscles were doing. I was so thirsty, I could not get enough water into me, but the damage had already been done. I somehow stumbled in for the last few holes, but shot some pretty big numbers. It was the oddest thing, one moment I felt fine, the next moment I thought I was going to hit the deck. It was because I had stopped drinking that I became dehydrated. So when you are going golfing, have something to drink before you go, then keep drinking all the way around the course. Hopefully, you will never have to experience the rubber legs that I felt.

Make sure in addition to drinking plenty of fluids, that you snack along the way. You need energy. Golf is much more tiring than anyone can imagine. Although it is important to snack, you need to munch on the right things. Pass on the candy and sweets if you can. They can do a number on your blood sugar, and make you more tired than the game makes you. Fruit is good, bananas, apples, dried fruit in little packets. Pretzels are another good choice. Dad's favorite is to put a few peanut butter and jelly sandwiches in his bag. He makes one for me, too. It is better to snack continually along the way, the same as drinking fluids, than have it all at once. That turkey sandwich, chips, pickles, and two sodas that you buy at the turn and finish before you putt out on #10 can only make you feel like you swallowed a bowling ball. It is best if you can eat before you go and maybe snack a tiny bit on the course.

We all know that too much caffeine can make you nervous and perhaps a little irritable, but did you know it can affect your golf, too? Being wired on caffeine can make you rush, hurt your tempo, and make it harder to make clear decisions on the course. At full caffeine throttle, you will run out of gas sooner than if you were not on it. I never realized how powerful caffeine is, but we learn a lot of things by accident. I learned this at a tournament in New Jersey. When we got to the course, there was a rain delay and it was pouring. My caddie and I went to the club house to shoot the breeze with the rest of the guys. It was cold and wet out, so we started drinking coffee. Lots of coffee. I didn't realize it, but I must have downed five cups of sludge, when they told us to get ready, we were playing. On the putting green, I couldn't make one from a foot, I was shaking so much. I thought I was getting sick or something until my caddie told me I had the coffee shakes. My tempo was all messed up that day, but I sure learned a good lesson. I still like coffee, but I have great respect for the caffeine in it. I like to mix decaf and regular, so I can adjust my caffeine intake and don't buzz myself into feeling tired. If I want a little pick me up in the afternoon, I will have a diet cola. Pay attention to your caffeine intake and adjust it to fit your needs. You may be quite surprised at how your tempo improves. You may also be surprised at how fresh you feel after playing a round.

Most of the seniors or near seniors I know spent a lot of time in the sun before sunscreen was invented. When I was a kid, we just got cooked and thought nothing of it. I am sure that I will pay for it someday, although my dermatologist tells me things look all right. The point is we can do something now that will help us. First of all, wear sunscreen at all times when you are outside. I use a number 30 greaseless, sweatproof, dry lotion that does not stain my clothes. Don't put on the sunscreen at the course, put it on before you leave home. Sunscreen needs at least a half an hour to be effective. Wear a hat. A wide brimmed hat is best, but be careful. Some wide brim golf hats have such a wide mesh that they don't keep much sun out. When buying a hat hold it under light and see how much gets through. If you can see much light, don't buy it and get a better one. If your skin is in bad shape, you can wear longsleeve shirts. Do whatever your doctor recommends. Golf is played out in the sun, so you need to be careful.

Lastly, while I'm on my safety kick, learn CPR (cardiopulmonary resuscitation). It is important that we know how to jump start a life in case one of our friends is dying in front of us. We can make a difference, but we must take the time to learn. One of my students is a paramedic who regularly revives people. He asked me if I knew CPR and I said no. Then he asked me to imagine how I would feel if someone I loved was dying in front of me, but I didn't know how to help them although I could have learned. I signed up for the course the next day. I can't think of a better gift you could give one of your friends than the gift of life if they need your help.

TO SUM IT UP

That about wraps up our chapter on some of the things that can ruin your game before you ever hit a ball. Don't fight your body's natural height and posture. If you are protecting your body after an injury, make the correct adjustments and swing slowly. Check with your doctor, and if she gives you permission, increase your flexibility with the home stretches. Warm up correctly so you can start playing better. Get plenty of rest, stay hydrated, and take care of yourself. If you are stressed or tired, lower your expectations. If you are under time pressure, putt instead of play. We have looked at things that can wreck your game, how about things that can help? This next chapter is a complete guide on what type of equipment can help you, and what is a waste of your money, so let's go.

How The Right Equipment Can Help

Whenever new students come to see me, I'm always curious to see what equipment they are carrying in their bag. Experience has shown me that most players don't have clubs that fit them or their swings. Many senior golfers are playing with old technology and not taking advantage of today's technology, which can improve your game. I can't help but recall the story of my own father, Harry. A few years back, dad decided after retiring to get pretty serious about his game. Up until then he had been playing a set of off-the-shelf clubs that he had bought some time ago at a sporting goods store. They were a good name brand, but they did not fit his 6'4" frame. It never really mattered, because he didn't play much, and his expectations were not very high. When dad started getting into it, we measured him and built him a set of graphite shafted irons and woods that fit perfectly. To this day he uses them and plays great, mid to low 80s with an occasional threat to the high 70s. The difference in his game after he started playing with those clubs was dramatic. I always ask him if he wants to try this or that, but his clubs have become a part of him, so he usually declines. Are you that attached to your clubs?

Are you absolutely sure they fit you? Do you look forward to hitting each and every club in your bag, or are there some clubs that no matter how hard you try they just don't work? It may not be all your fault. Some of the blame may fall on clubs that either don't fit you or are simply not matched to your swing correctly. Our task is to make sure that our equipment is not holding us back from playing better, which is often the case. If there is a club in your bag that you don't look forward to using, then it should not be in there. It should either be replaced by something you can use, or not replaced at all, just taken out. Wouldn't it be fun to like all of your clubs?

What we will do in this chapter is take a look at equipment and how it can help the senior swing. One of the added benefits of my job as a P.G.A. professional and instructor is that I have the good fortune to try different clubs as I teach. I sometimes hit demonstration shots to get a point across, and many students ask me to hit their clubs so I can give them my opinion. What a blessing. There are not many clubs that anyone can ask me about without me being informed. Believe it or not, no matter how many clubs I hit, and no matter how good they feel, nobody's feel as good as mine do in my hands. The reason for this is simple, THEY FIT ME. As a professional, I pride myself on being able to hit just about anything, but if you picked up my clubs, chances are they would feel uncomfortable to you. They are ½" over modern standard length, which is 1" over traditional standard, swing weighted to D-5, tipped ½ way in between R+S flex, 1° upright lie angle, with two extra wraps under a .58 tour wrap grip. This may sound like a secret missile launch code, but before this chapter is over you will understand what all this means.

According to all of the clubs we fit for students, less than 10% fit into what has been historically considered a "standard" set of golf clubs. Back before we knew better, a golfer would go into a store, and the salesman, who also worked in the fishing department, would see what he had in stock. Whatever the verdict from the stock room was would determine what clubs you would be playing for a while. Those days are pretty much gone. Now, most of the golf stores have an educated, professional, sales staff made up of people who are interested in making sure you have the right equipment in your hands. The world of retail golf is very competitive, so shops must have satisfied customers if they are to stay in business. You really can't go wrong if you buy your equipment from a reputable golf shop, on or off the course.

Let's look at some of the options when you are going to buy clubs. We see the advertisements on the television of many different clubs claiming to be the best. How can they all be the best? Will they work for you like they work for the pros? Can they really improve your game? Are they worth paying that much money for them? Let's try to sort this out.

First of all, we need to set a few things straight. All of the major manufacturers make very fine clubs of excellent quality. They can help your game, but they must fit you. At most good shops or clubs, you can take them out and demo them, which is very important. If you buy a set of clubs without trying them out first, you could be making a big mistake. Some of the equipment on the market is very expensive. Students are forever asking me if a particular driver is worth $400 or not. My answer is if it works that well for you, and you think it is worth it, it is. Obviously, you need to be able to afford this type of equipment to buy it. Again, it must fit you and you must demo it first. If you can, you should try it at a range or on the course. If you must hit into a net, many places have swing speed and ball flight computers to assist you. Get as much education as you can before investing in a set of clubs. P.G.A. professionals are experts in equipment and club fitting, so whenever possible seek their advice.

So do you have to take out a mortgage to get a good set of clubs? Not if you don't want to. Here is another option in your search for the perfect sticks. It's called custom club fitting and is rapidly becoming a very popular way to get clubs. It sounds like it costs megabucks, but it doesn't. I'll explain.

When I opened my golf school and shop, I had some major decisions to make concerning golf clubs. I knew my students trust my judgment, so I had to get the right combination of equipment in the shop. I looked at all the possibilities. Many of my students are senior golfers on fixed incomes, so I needed clubs that would be affordable for all to buy. I do carry the major brands, but I knew I needed an option for those who found a $400 driver a little steep. I also would not feel comfortable selling "clones" of the major clubs. Many are low quality, and some are even illegal due to copyright fraud. I wasn't about to get involved with that. I had to be able to custom fit all my customers with quality clubs at a reasonable price. I finally settled on Chicago brand club heads. They make a great stainless steel club head of their own design at a good price. I then take top grade shafts and grips, and have a superb club, custom fitted, that doesn't empty my students' bank accounts. I play the same clubs that I sell and am amazed at how good they feel. I am more than a little embarrassed to think that I too bought clubs without being fitted or trying them out way back when. I made myself a set these clubs and now they are my favorite clubs of all time.

Please don't misunderstand me. There is nothing wrong with the name brand clubs. They are all fine products. I have accounts with these companies for the students who want only those clubs. I custom fit my students for those clubs too. The major companies are getting into custom fitting more every day, too. This makes me very happy. In a few years, I don't know that you will be able to just walk in and buy a set of clubs without being fitted, which will be great for the consumer.

As we will learn, there are 11 club-fitting variables to be taken into consideration, with some being more important than others. Now suppose we have decided that we want a set of custom-fitted clubs. Where do we go and what should we look for? First, find someone in your area whom you can trust, perhaps a P.G.A. professional or professional club maker who has his own shop and makes his own clubs. Ask a lot of questions (we will find out what to ask), and get recommendations from other customers. Here is the topper. You should be able to get a custom set of irons with some top grade steel shafts for about half of what the big name brands go for. If they are properly fitted, they will feel as good as any club at any price. On the other hand, try not to fall for the super bargain set either. The club head must be stainless steel or titanium, not a zinc composite. Stainless has that crisp click and is very durable. You can test the head by using a magnet to see if it's stainless steel. If the magnet sticks, then the club head is steel. The steel shafts should be a name brand, and a good grade, True Temper, Apollo, Brunswick, to name a few. The grades in steel shafts differ dramatically in feel and quality, but not by much money. If you can upgrade to a better shaft for a few dollars more, by all means do it. There are many catalogs that describe shafts, their performance characteristics and approximate price.

How about graphite? In my opinion, graphite shafts are one of the greatest things to come along for seniors since the early bird dinner. They are lighter, so you can generate more club head speed. You can feel the club head better. Graphite also has fabulous shock absorption capabilities, especially on off-center hits. There is one catch. You need to get a decent graphite shaft, and they are more expensive than steel shafts. Rest assured when you see an advertisement for a complete set of graphite-shafted woods and irons for $199, they are probably not of good quality. These can snap, as we often see in our repair facility. Also there is a good chance these will not be very consistent through the set. What this means is that your eight iron may be regular flex, your six iron may be ladies flex, and your four iron stiff flex. This explains why students sometime tell me, "I hit all my irons well except my nine and six." You would probably be better off getting a set with good quality lightweight steel shafts than cheap low quality graphite that don't do what they are supposed to.

Some of today's steel shafts are featuring shock absorption systems. I am sure this trend will continue until a standard steel shaft is a thing of the past. The new ones just feel too good. They are really making great strides in both steel and graphite shaft technology. So whether you go with major name brand clubs or the less expensive, not so heavily advertised brands, get good shafts and have them fitted for you. Believe me, you will feel a difference.

Woods come in several different materials. Many of the woods on the low end of the price range are alloy heads. Lately I have been seeing some of my range customers showing up with what they think is a titanium club and commenting on the fact that it only cost $39.95. When I read the bottom, it says, "Aluminum titanium alloy." I would stay away from these if I could, keeping in mind that you always get what you pay for. This is a favorite trick of some inexpensive manufacturers. They mark their club heads with something like "Aluminum titanium alloy." They only put a speck of titanium in the head, which doesn't do a thing. All the consumer sees is the word titanium, and buys it. Most of the cheap alloy heads feel dead at impact, as if there was something foreign on the club face. Stainless steel heads are only slightly more expensive and worth it. I would prefer to see you with one quality stainless steel head wood than a whole set of zinc composite alloy woods. You will again feel the difference.

I still see a few real wood-headed woods show up at my school once in a while. The only way I would recommend these is if you are an extremely fine ball striker, use balata golf balls, hate metal woods, really don't care how far you hit it, or a combination of any of the above. Real wood club heads are harder to hit, less forgiving, require maintenance and just don't hit as far. You'll notice that you would have to look hard on the senior tour to find a real wood head. That leaves us with titanium and stainless steel again. I have played both for a long time and have come up with this advice for my students. I did not realize much extra yardage with my titanium wood. It felt great, but so does my oversize stainless steel wood, which is what I use now. Stainless technology has gotten to where they can make a quality club head the same size as the jumbo titanium clubs at ¼ of the cost. Am I saying not to buy your favorite brand of titanium wood? Of course not, if you can afford one. But if a $400 driver is not in your budget, don't worry, you can hit it just as far with a top-quality jumbo stainless steel driver if it has the right shaft for you. A club of this kind, with a good graphite shaft should go around $100. That saves a lot more money for greens fees.

What about this titanium stuff anyway? Titanium is a very light, very strong, and very expensive metal. It allowed club manufacturers to make clubs long, light, and big. It is important to understand that it is the length and lightness of the club that adds distance, not titanium alone. Shortly after the original titanium driver came out, the craziness began. Everything needed to say titanium or no one would buy it. It's like a magic word, this titanium. Luckily, even the major manufacturers are doing a lot more in stainless steel. I am glad for that, because it's hard for some golfers to afford clubs that expensive, yet they feel they are missing something. By the way, I'm hoping for a titanium toothbrush for my birthday. I hear you can brush your teeth in six seconds flat.

I have some advice that I think will help. If you find a driver that you like, and you hit it consistently, stop looking. I see students all the time who have been hitting the ball great with a club change for the sake of getting three more yards off the tee. The next thing you know they're hitting it farther all right, but the last twenty yards is in the pond. We all get caught up in the search to hit it farther and straighter, often overlooking one major point. Golf clubs and balls are regulated by the United States Golf Association. The technology exists today for manufacturers to build a driver and ball combination that would produce 400-yard tee shots consistently. It is just not approved for play and so we golfers being the fine upstanding ladies and gents that we are wouldn't think of destroying the integrity of the game by buying illegal clubs or balls. But if it is legal and during tests averaged 2.3 feet longer than your driver, it's worth $500 easily. We are a funny bunch, aren't we? That reminds me, I'm just about due for a driver change. After all, it has been a whole year.

Where do we find these quality clubs at reasonable prices? We need to shop around. Here are some questions to ask. What are the credentials of the people doing the fitting? How long have they been doing this? You can ask the pro or builder who the club head manufacturer is. Are they stainless steel or an alloy? What type of shaft do they recommend? Who will build them? Who will fit them? What is the warranty? How long does it take to get? Where can you demo these clubs? You want to find someone you can trust, maybe someone who comes highly recommended. P.G.A. professionals, members of the Professional Clubmakers Society, or members of the Golf Clubmakers Association should be your first choice, as they have gone through extensive training in this field.

Many golfers don't realize the importance of a grip that fits. When your grip fits correctly, your two middle fingers on your left hand should be close to or lightly touching your hand. Check your grips and make sure they fit your hands. If your grip is too small, it will result in excessive hand action. Conversely, if your grip is too big you will tend to hold on too tightly and not release the club. Grips can be made to fit your hand correctly by either building up the shaft with masking tape, or in rare cases of extremely small hands, by stretching the grip as it is put on to make it smaller. Since some of you have not had the opportunity to watch grips being put on, I'll explain it to you. The old grip is cut off with a razor knife. The shaft is cleaned, any build-up tape is put on to get the grip to the desired thickness, and then a two-sided tape is put on for the length of the grip. Solvent is squirted into the new grip to coat the inside. Any excess is dribbled onto the taped club which is now snugly held in a vice. The new grip is then slid on because the solvent has made the tape slippery. The grip is then aligned properly and let dry. When the solvent evaporates, you have a bond that will hold up to just about anything. Getting your clubs regripped can make them feel new again. You should also wash your grips once in a while. Use dish detergent and a soft brush, make sure you rinse them thoroughly; we don't want any soap residue left on the grip. If you have arthritis, check out some of the arthritic grips on the market, they are really neat. These grips are much larger than standard, and many have roughed up surfaces to help you hold on. You can pretty much disregard fitting instructions if you are getting arthritic grips. They should feel big. That is how they are designed so you don't have to squeeze to the point of pain to hold onto your club. I know these work. Some of my students with arthritis tell me they could not play without them and that's good enough for me.

CLUB FITTING VARIABLES

Fitting a set of clubs can be as simple or involved as you want. I think there is a point where it can become almost overly technical, too. Here are the variables taken into consideration when fitting a set of clubs:

1. Shaft material - steel or graphite.
2. Head material - stainless or titanium.
3. Club head design - oversize, jumbo, standard size, midsize
4. Club lofts - the angle of trajectory that the clubs produce.
5. Club length - how long your clubs should be.
6. Lie angle - how the club soles on the ground at address and impact.
7. Swing weight and total weight - how heavy are they and how heavy do they feel
8. Shaft flex - the "spring" in the shaft.
9. Grip size - how a grip fits your hand
10. Set make up - what clubs a person needs for his set.
11. Face angle on woods - whether the face on a wood is square, open or closed at address

The clubs you have now may or may not fit you. In my shop, as well as any reputable pro shop, we check students' clubs free of charge. Educating yourself can only help you understand how the correct clubs can work for you. If you know your clubs fit you, it instills confidence when you play. It may sound funny, but my clubs fit me so well that if I hit a bad shot I know for sure that it's not the club's fault, although I sure would like to use that excuse now and again. Can you say that about your clubs? Let's go through these variables one by one so we can learn more about the clubs we depend on to enjoy our games.

Shaft material - A pretty simple choice. Do we want steel or graphite? Some golfers will mix and match. They will put graphite in their woods and steel in their irons. Some will go all graphite or all steel. You make the call after trying some different shafts and seeing what feels good to you. Keep in mind that graphite is more expensive.

Head material - Stainless steel or titanium. Even if you opt for titanium in your woods, your irons are still probably going to be stainless steel. Again, pick a reputable manufacturer and if you can afford to, stay away from alloy heads. Some of the newer heads have inserts of another metal, but I really haven't felt enough difference to justify the extra cost.

Club head design - If you find a good quality club head manufacturer then you need to find a club head that feels and looks good to you. Perimeter weighting has changed the design of irons forever. If you are anything but a single-digit handicap, and still play the old blade clubs, you need to try perimeter-weighted irons (Figure 3.1) These are irons where the weight has been taken from behind the sweet spot and added to the edges of the club. The result is a club that is much more forgiving on off-center hits, is easier to get air-

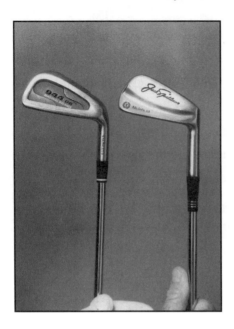

Figure 3.1. Perimeter weighted cavity-back irons (shown at left) are much more forgiving on mis-hits than the older style blades.

borne, and has a much bigger sweet spot. One of the professionals who taught me a great deal in my career told me once that when you stand over a club for the first time you can tell if you like it just by looking at it. If it pleases the eye, and it's fit right for you, it should improve your game. In the irons, it's the top line that catches your eye. Do you prefer a thick or thin top line? Some like a standard size club head, some midsize, and some feel oversize fits their needs. Experiment until you find an iron that you stand over and say "I like the looks of this club." This is obviously the first step in feeling confident about your equipment. Visually it's got to appeal to you.

In the woods, the choices are also almost unlimited. Do you like the jumbo woods, or a traditional size wood; steel, wood, or titanium? It's also a good idea to find out if that same design that you like in a driver is also available in fairway woods. Make sure it is available in the lofts that you want. Offset woods are making a comeback. These are woods that have the hosel out in front of the club face. The design theory is to keep your hands out in front of the ball and clubhead at impact, thereby preventing a slice. Some golfers love their offset woods, other have a hard time looking at them after playing traditional clubs during their career. The best thing to do is try one if you think you are interested.

Lofts - today's lofts on irons tend to be a little stronger than they used to be. Hit some and see if you like the trajectory. On the woods is where the lofts are most important. We will discuss wood lofts later in this chapter. The object is to try many different lofts until you find the one that hits the farthest, but you can still control.

Length - Here is where we have to be very careful. Depending on your arm length in comparison to your height, you could need anything from an inch or two below standard to an inch or two above. If the club is too long, it's very difficult to get the clubs to lie correctly on the ground. Most of the time if I see students with too long a club, they are gripping down to make the club work. The worst scenario is a club that is too short. This is another topped shot waiting to happen. You are forced out of your natural hitting height by a club that's too short, and you start bent over more than you should be. We will learn what can happen from here. On the back swing we stand up to our natural height. Then it's back down to the ball so we can find out if we got lucky or not. What a shame. I see this occur with ladies more often than men. Many standard ladies sets are just too short for today's women. When our club length is correct, we should be standing rather tall. There will be more bend in our back than our knees and the sole of the club head should be lying flat on the ground (Figure 3.2). Remember, if you like everything about your present clubs, but feel they are too long or short for you, get them checked by someone reputable. They can be extended or shortened to fit without emptying your wallet.

Figure 3.2. A properly fitted golf club will complement a good posture that has more bend at the waist than the knees.

Lie angle - The lie angle is how flat the club sits on the ground when you address the ball. Your divots can give you feedback on how your club is coming into the ball. Your divot should be even in depth, not toe deep or heel deep. What I often see is the combination of a club that is too long and too upright a lie angle. When the club is soled at address, the toe is sticking up. With the toe sticking up, the sweet spot is effectively cut in half. It makes it almost impossible to get the ball airborne as it feeds the ball into the hosel often. Check your lie angle.

Swing weight and total weight -Total weight of the club is just that, how much a club weighs. It is determined by the weight of the components. This is where a club can really affect the senior swing. If a club is too heavy for someone to handle, she can't generate the club head speed that she could if she had a lighter club. This is why graphite is such a good thing for many ladies and seniors. They are able to swing the club faster and hit it farther in many cases and club head feel is enhanced. Is a heavier club ever better for anyone?

Yes, in some instances. Sometimes I fit either very strong men and ladies or golfers who swing very fast. Both would be candidates for steel shafts. The extra weight of the steel will slow down the fast swingers and smooth them out. The very strong players have the potential to damage graphite shafts, so I warn them beforehand. One of the best tests you can do is hit demo clubs that are alike except one is steel shafted and the other graphite. This will tell you what you need to know about total weight and what's best for you.

Swing weight is a whole different thing and is confusing to many golfers. This has to do with the weight relationship of the head to the rest of the club and how it feels. On a swing weight scale, the club's balance is given a numerical designation. This is transposed to a chart that gives your club a "swing weight" of a letter and number like D-1. Generally, the lower the swing weight, the harder it is to feel the club head. Some of the newer technology has very light overall or real weight, but a relatively heavy swing weight for more feel. Your clubs should be matched pretty closely in swing weight to feel similar. If you like the weight of your clubs and they are swing weighted to similar readings, then they will all feel good to you.

Shaft flex - This is a huge one, especially for seniors. Many of the seniors whom I talk with are playing a shaft flex that does not correspond to their swing speed. The shaft flex must be correct or the club will be difficult to hit. Too whippy tends to hook, too stiff tends to slice and feel hard to hit. There are five mainstream shaft flexes, they are L flex, A flex, R flex, S flex, X flex, with L being the most flexible, X being tour pro stiff, and the others falling proportionally in between. A club builder can also make your clubs in between any flex, as we often do in our shop. One thing is for sure. Most golfers are playing shafts that are way too stiff for them. Some call it a macho thing, but I always consider it a lack of education.

One of my favorite tricks is to let people hit clubs and not tell them what shaft is in the club until they are finished. Often the shaft they hit the best surprises them because it is an entire flex softer than they are currently hitting. How a correctly fitted shaft works is important to your swing and the results you will see. A properly fitted shaft will load and unload at the correct time in your swing. You will get maximum distance and accuracy with an effortless swing. Maybe one of the most important benefits is the consistency you will develop. If you are swinging within yourself, and have been doing so with a particular club that fits you, your tendency to try to kill your shot is greatly reduced. These shaft flexes are determined by swing speed and feel. Generally speaking, L or ladies flex is for swing speeds up to about 65 mph. An A flex or senior flex shaft is good up to about 75 mph. R or regular flex works up to about 85 mph. S flex or stiff is used up to around 100 mph. X flex or tour stiff is 100 mph plus. The reason that I am using approximate speeds is that again today's club fitting can fine tune all of these for your exact speed. Regardless of how many magazine articles and technical journals we read, nothing takes the place of feel. Hit the same club with different shaft flexes and see which one gives you the best combination of distance and accuracy.

This also applies to the loft on woods. I joke around all the time that if I could magically change one thing in golf, it would be to take the low lofted drivers out of everyone's bags except the pros. Think about it, the club you get into the most trouble with is your driver. It probably has between 9° and 10.5° loft. You could use a three wood off the tee and hit it straight all day. Yet for those few extra yards we are willing to hit it into the rough or worse. My favorite demo clubs that we carry for seniors are 11° and 13° drivers with 44" graphite A flex shafts. It is rare that a student tries one of these clubs and doesn't hit it significantly farther than their present driver. The reason is the added loft. It helps get the ball into the air faster and carries it farther. Also, the higher the loft, the more back spin it produces. Back spin counteracts side spin, which is responsible for slices and hooks. You should try a demo driver in a higher loft (11°,12°,13°) whenever you can. You won't regret it. You will be able to hit many more greens if you can find your tee shot.

My motto is "If I can find it, I can hit it again." This is going to be one of our keys to playing better. We need a perfect club to hit off the tee. It has got to be one that combines both respectable distance and accuracy enough to find many fairways. This is not always the driver that you hit the longest. I myself have a driver that I hit a long way. What makes me the happiest is that I hit it straighter than any other driver I've ever had. I'm sure that I could find one that hits it another three yards, but it is the accuracy that enables me to play well. I can hit greens if my tee shot is in the fairway. It's tough to make par from hazards.

Another trend is to build drivers extra long. It always makes me chuckle that we as golfers will always take a good idea and push it way past its intended usefulness. A good case in point is driver length. Standard length on drivers was 43". Then came the graphite and titanium revolution and this was extended to 44". This was perfectly acceptable because the shaft-club head combination was lighter and easier to use. The end result was a club that hit the ball longer for those who already knew how to drive the ball adequately.

What happened next boggles the mind. I see clubs being advertised at 48" and 52" lengths. They guarantee longer tee shots. Even the pros who endorse them can't believe the distance. It's a miracle. That's until you try to keep the ball in play. I get asked to take these clubs on trade in all the time. When I ask why they want to get rid of them, the answer is always the same, "I catch it once in a while, but all the other times I hit it off the world." They forgot to tell you that the pro who hits it farther already had the most perfect golf swing you ever saw. If you're going to get one of these babies working for you, make sure you have a perfect swing to start with.

A good rule of thumb is that today's standard length graphite shafted driver is around 44" long. If your current driver is 44", and you hit it down the middle most of the time but want to hit it farther, then a longer one might help you. If you have a 44" driver and spray it all over the place, a longer one will only help you spray it farther into trouble. The number one objective of getting a driver is to find one that you can hit well most of the time. A bad tee shot courtesy of a wild driver will have you playing catch up all day long.

We need to remember a few basic principles. The longer a club, the longer the ball will fly. The longer the ball flies, the more apt it is to find trouble. It comes back to that backspin, side spin thing. If you hit the ball 150 yards off the tee, than an extra long driver with the correct loft may help you gain a few yards. But if you hit it solidly off the tee now, don't go longer if it will sacrifice your control. My best advice is to try different clubs until you find the right one and stick with it.

One of my amateur friends was playing very well for a while a few years back. I couldn't help but notice that he was hitting his tee shots longer but also much straighter than ever before. This allowed him to hit more greens, not take any penalties from errant tee shots, and even on holes he could not reach, he would lay up and let his brilliant short game take over. After some interrogation he reluctantly showed me his new driver, as if it were a crime that he wasn't hitting a "pro" lofted driver. It was 12°and 43½". I'll never forget how well he played using that club. He didn't change his swing, he only got a club that complemented his ability and strength level. That club built so much confidence in him that to this day he is fearless off the tee, whereas before he never looked forward to his tee shots.

Back to our variables. Face angle has kind of gone out of style and doesn't really apply to us any more. When they built real wood clubs, they could make the club square, open, or closed depending on your wishes. The problem with this is that it only put a bandage on the wound, but didn't heal it. They tried this with a few metal woods, but these woods are easier to hit to begin with. Changing the face angle overcompensated for the swing errors they were designed to correct. Plus, now it's easier to fix your swing.

The last variable is extremely important to senior golfers. It is set make up. This is where we determine what clubs we will carry in our bag. We need to be honest with ourselves when we answer the following questions. How strong are we? Realistically, what is the strongest part of our game? How long are the courses we play? How much do we want to spend? We will go over some different scenarios to find these answers out.

In my experience, it takes a certain amount of swing speed to get a long iron airborne. If you are, after getting measured, going to be using A or L flex shafts, then a 1,2,3 and even 4 iron should probably never be in your bag. These require a tremendous amount of club head speed and precision to get in the air. Instead, you could use 3, 5, 7, even 9 woods and then have 5,6,7,8,9, pw, sw and lob wedge to really help you score. If you play longer courses, you could add a 11° or 13° 44" driver to that set. If you are fitted to R flex shafts, go with 10° or 11° driver, 3,5,7 woods and then 4,5,6,7,8,9, pw, sw and lob wedge. For S flex and low handicappers, pretty much anything goes. Since I personally have always enjoyed playing the long irons, and play them well, I carry a 9.5° driver and 1,2,3,4,5,6,7,8,9, pw, sw and lob wedge. An odd set indeed, but that's the beauty of making up a set that fits your game. As long as you don't exceed fourteen clubs as per the rules of golf, anything goes if it fits your game.

Bear in mind another thing. Even though the rules of golf state that you must not exceed 14 clubs to play with, that doesn't mean that every golfer has to have 14 clubs in their bag. Occasionally I'll pull a 3 or 4 iron out of one of my student's bags and it looks brand new, not even a scratch on it. They carry it in their bag just in case they lose all common sense and feel the need to be humbled instantly. They would be much better leaving those clubs in the closet. Then we wouldn't be tempted to hit them in a moment of brainlessness. Look at it this way. If professionals hit their irons with a 10- to 12-yard difference in distance between each one, then you may be only seeing six yards difference if you use an A or L flex shaft. As you get to the longer irons, that gap will close, so often your 3,4, and 5 will go the same distance. If this happens to you, it's time to take out the long irons and bring on the fairway woods. Try 5, 7, and 9 woods until you find ones that are easier to hit than your long irons. Fairway woods are much friendlier and fun to hit. They have more mass in the club head and don't require as much precision or speed to get in the air. They are also more versatile.

Notice that in all of the sets I recommend a pitching wedge, sand wedge and a lob wedge. The reason is that we must have a razor sharp short game and need every tool available to accomplish this. In the following chapters we will talk about the short game, as this is a place where seniors can really cut some strokes off their scores. The lofts on these wedges should be spread apart enough that you can tell the difference. For instance if your pitching wedge is 50°, then your sand wedge should be 55° and your lob wedge should be around 60°. Be careful not to have the lofts too close together. My 55° sand wedge matches the head design of the rest of my irons. My 60° wedge is a bounce wedge that is great out of the bunker and for high, soft shots around the green. Find a group of wedges you like. We will be using them often.

Putters are a big issue. When buying a putter, you need to know how to hold it correctly to see if it fits. We will discuss putters in depth after we learn the correct way to grip and set up to them in the short game section.

The bottom line is that the rules have changed when it comes to buying equipment. Try things out, get good advice from a reputable source, and get a set of clubs that fits your swing and your game. It's not how much you spend, it's how your clubs work for you that counts.

OTHER EQUIPMENT

Golf balls have also changed for the better recently. Now we have many options to choose from and again, we want a ball that fits our game. Seniors were really never given much consideration by the ball companies, but that has also changed. Once again, with the proper information, we should be able to pick a ball that is right for us.

First off, if you are a beginner, expect to lose a lot of balls. This is part of learning where not to hit it. I never recommend that beginners buy new golf balls, as this is not very cost effective. You can get a bag of balls that scuba divers have fished out of ponds for less than half what you would pay for new ones. An added benefit to this is that you get to try out the many different brands to find one you like. As you get better, you can start to buy new balls.

Balls have spin rates and compression ratings that vary. Spin rate is obviously how much a ball spins when it's hit. The compression rating is how soft or hard the ball is and how it compresses on the club face at impact. If you use A or L flex shafts, you swing at less than 75 mph and a lower compression ball would work well for you. What happens in theory is a lower compression ball will compress then spring off the club face, giving you added zip. An 80 compression ball would be ideal for you. Some don't actually have the rating on the box, but chances are if it says specially made for seniors or ladies, it's around an 80 compression ball. Anyone that is using R or S flex shafts should use one of the high spin distance balls on the market. What wonderful pieces of technology these balls are. They come off the club face like a rocket, yet spin enough to stop on the green and feel soft in our short game.

I feel some golfers actually lose their scoring capabilities with some of the distance only balls on the market. You may get a few extra yards out of them, but when you hit the green, they roll off the back. My dad and I experimented with this a few years ago. He actually scored worse with a distance only ball because they would not hold on the green, just rolled off the back into trouble. Then we switched him to a spin and distance ball and he scored much better. If you really don't hit it far enough to hit a green in regulation, a distance ball won't magically make up that much difference, however a ball with more spin will help when you are trying to pitch it close. Ball technology is changing faster than the weather, so don't be afraid to experiment to find a ball that suits your game. The beauty of trying different golf balls is that you can't make a mistake that will cost you a lot of money. You can try a sleeve at a time, and if you don't like them, you haven't lost much.

The spikeless revolution is sweeping the nation. Metal spikes will soon be a thing of the past at most courses. Many senior golfers that I know have been wearing nonmetal spike systems for years. They find it amusing that the rest of the golfing world is finally discovering what they have known for years; for comfort and convenience, nonmetal spikes can't be beat. What are some of the benefits of nonmetal spikes? First of all, you can put on your golf shoes at home, drive to the course, and get out of your car ready to play. When you get done playing, you can go anywhere you would like and not have to change your shoes again. What a wonderful convenience! Since it is very hard to drag your feet with nonmetal spikes on, I have observed tremendous improvement in the overall quality of the greens at the clubs that have gone spikeless. I have found it much easier to walk, which prevents the occasional stumble I have experienced in the past. Here is another benefit you may not know. The metal spikes have occasionally worked themselves free of golfers' shoes and are left on the golf course. Along comes the maintenance crew with their very expensive lawn mowers and, BAM, they hit one of these loose spikes. Not only can it be shot out like a bullet, but it ruins the blade on the mower. They then need to take the mower apart, fix or replace the blade, then put it back together again. As you can see, this costs time and money, and the golfers pay for it in either greens fees or dues. The nonmetal spikes just get mulched in the mowers. As you can see, there are many benefits to using non metal spikes, but are there drawbacks? Let's take a look.

When the early spikeless systems came out, they lacked one major benefit of metal spikes, superior traction. After using spikes all of my life, I found myself slipping around with the nonmetal spikes that were available. There is good news now. Like most other industries, the nonmetal spike research has continued, and they are getting better every day. The traction is far better than the early versions. I am sure that this technology will contine to advance, but in the interim we must keep one thing in mind. No matter what brand of nonmetal spike you use, they won't afford the same traction as the old metal spikes in certain conditions. There is information on the packaging, but the most obvious area of concern is a wet, slippery slope next to the green or tee. I think if you follow the instructions and exercise caution, the benefits of nonmetal spikes greatly outweigh the detriments.

Do you wear a golf glove? Some golfers just don't like the feel, but many don't wear gloves because they wear out too quickly and it gets expensive. This does not have to happen. As we will see in the grip section, most gloves wear out because the club either rides too high up in the palm crease of our left hand or we are holding the club too far out on the end. Both of these scenarios cause friction and will wear holes in your glove. But the smart thing to do is overcome these faults and take advantage of the positive effects a glove can have on our swing. So what does a glove actually do? Our hands contain natural oils and perspiration. A glove forms a barrier between our skin and the grip, giving us more control. The most important benefit of a glove is the effect it has on our grip pressure. The added traction allows us to soften up our grip and make a more tension-free swing. If you have especially weak hands, I would even try wearing a glove on each hand.

Naturally, gloves are another item with a huge selection to choose from. There are basically three types of glove. The first is all leather. Most are a fine cabretta quality, but can vary in thickness.

The thinner ones are most expensive, offer superb feel, but wear out quickly. If value is an issue, this is not the glove for you. The thicker, all-leather gloves are more durable, don't cost as much, and still provide good feel. The only draw back of the all-leather gloves is they are not good in hot, humid weather or rain. Getting them wet can ruin them. Our second glove choice is the synthetic glove. These are made from a material that feels similar to leather, just not as rich. These gloves are much better than no glove at all, but can get hot because they don't breathe like real leather. These are great for the budget minded and sell for about half the price of an all-leather glove. The third option is the newest addition to the glove lineup. It is a combination of synthetic and leather. This glove features top-quality leather on the palm and fingers where you hold the club, but the rest is synthetic. It is more durable and less expensive than the all-leather gloves, but provides better feel than the synthetic gloves. This glove breathes nicely, so it doesn't feel sticky in hot weather. Choose a glove that fits your needs and your budget. When you find a glove that you like, buy two and rotate them when you play. Wear them on alternate holes, so they have a chance to dry out in between holes. When you are finished playing, let your glove air dry . Do not stuff it in your golf bag pocket or there's a good chance it will feel crunchy and hard the next time you dig it out. Gloves will help the senior swing, so get a good grip and try one on.

There are some great gadgets that I have found to help senior golfers. One of them is a putter ball pick up. This is a little suction cup that goes on the end of your putter. When you hole out your putt, you simply turn your putter up side down, stick it in the hole, and out comes your ball. It saves your back for better things and my students who have these absolutely love them. The ball pick up should be made of rubber and sell for less than $4.00. Stay away from the plastic ones. They don't work as well.

If you play a course that you like to walk, you should buy a pull cart. Even a light carry bag can cause stress on your shoulder if you carry it. Renting a pull cart is not very cost effective when you could buy one and have it pay for itself after a while. When you go to buy a pull cart, get a good one. If it has rivets instead of bolts it will probably not last as long. If a rivet pops from the weight of your bag, you may not be able to get it fixed. If it has nuts and bolts, it is usually made better and if it does break, it is easily fixed. A good sturdy pull cart can carry lots of other stuff too. You can personalize it to carry a water bottle for your favorite beverage, score card holder, pencils, extra balls, and more. Many of the better brands are fully collapsible and fit into the trunk of your car with your bag. Get a good cart, customize it, splash on some sunscreen, wear your hat, and enjoy your walk in the park.

During your walk in the park, you might find your ball in a water hazard. A good ball retriever will save you money on balls. I recommend the type with butterfly wires on the end. This kind you just lay on the top of the ball and the middle wire traps it. The retrievers with the little cup on the end are harder to use than a 1 iron off of a tight lie. It is bad enough that we hit a ball into the drink, but we don't want to add insult to injury by not being able to use our ball retriever quickly and effectively. Get a good one that is easy to use.

With all the new technology available for seniors, there is probably something out there that can help you enjoy the game more. Hopefully, with what you have learned in this chapter, you will be able to make a more educated decision on what may help you. If you get stuck, or have a question, ask your local P.G.A. professional for advice, that's what we are here for.

Now that we know what equipment we can use, let's learn how to use it correctly. In the following chapters we will look at the senior swing, its possibilities and limitations. We will learn how to hit it long, what makes it go straight, short game technique, and some great tricks for senior golfers. It sounds like a good plan, so let's go.

A Foundation of Basic Fundamentals

I n this chapter we will explore the basic functions of the senior swing and how they affect us. We will be able to build a solid foundation for a swing that will repeat over and over again, even under pressure. Will everyone have the exact same swing motion? Of course not, as we are all individuals with different levels of flexibility and strength. We will adjust our swing to fit our own body. It is true, however, that the basic fundamentals should be very similar from swing to swing. As any professional will tell you, there is no substitute for good fundamentals. We all occasionally bumble our way through a practice session and blame our hooks and slices on a lack of brain power; however, that is rarely the actual cause of our swing distress. The real problem can usually be traced back to a breakdown in one of the basics: grip, aim, or setup. Let's discuss the grip first.

THE GRIP

Senior golfers need an especially sound grip assembly. If our grip is seated correctly in our hands, we will not have to hold the club as tightly. By keeping our hands soft we will be able to create more whipping action, and hence more distance. The grip is a major component of a good golf swing. I like to explain it to my students with this example. Suppose we took a brand new car and installed a broken transmission. No matter how beautiful the car looked, it would not be reliable. Consider your grip the transmission of your golf swing. I have not seen anyone with a bad grip play well; in fact I have seen many good swing motions ruined by a faulty transmission.

I'd like to take time now to explain the five most common grip faults I see. They are:

GRIP FAULT NUMBER 1 = GRIPPING TOO FAR OUT ON THE END OF THE CLUB. There should be at least ¼" of the butt of the club sticking out of the back of your left hand.

This creates counter balance and you are able to control the club. Many golfers come into my shop to get a new glove because their old glove has a hole worn in the palm pad. Only friction could cause a hole like this, and friction is caused by movement. If that much friction is being created when you swing, your club must be moving in your hand as you swing. This will result in off center hits and loss of control. Your mind tries to tell you that you will gain more distance if you grip way out beyond the end, but as you can see, the exact opposite is true. Think of when you hold a hammer. To create the proper counter balance, you would never hold it out past the end, would you? If you did, it would wobble in your hand and you would experience a loss of control, the same as if you hold the club too far out on the end. So grip down ¼", gain control, and even save some money on gloves. (Figure 4.1)

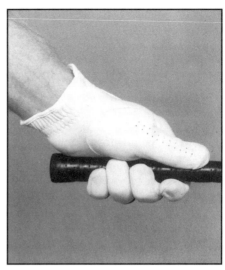

Figure 4.1. Gripping down on the club ¼" will give you more control and save wear and tear on your gloves.

GRIP FAULT NUMBER 2= HAVING THE GOLF CLUB RIDE UP IN THE CREASE OF YOUR LEFT HAND. This is a definite swing killer. On your left hand, the club must be seated under the palm pad and across the line where the fingers meet the hand. If it rides up into the crease of your left hand you will experience complete loss of control. You will lose club head rotation and will need a death grip just to keep the club from flying out of your hands. As you can see, this is not a very good fault to have. Your hands and left forearm get sore and you run the risk of launching the club farther than the ball. Not a shot that builds a lot of confidence. (Figure 4.2). This problem often occurs when we set the club head on the ground as we get our grip. We will be holding the club in the air as we get our grip, but I will explain this in more depth later in this chapter.

GRIP FAULT NUMBER 3 = HAVING A BIG GAP BETWEEN YOUR LEFT THUMB AND FOREFINGER. We know your left thumb should be slightly offset to the right of the center line on the golf club grip. The problem is when there is a gap be-

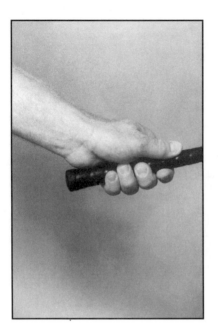

Figure 4.2. The grip must be under the palm pad on the left hand if we are to control the club at a high rate of speed.

tween the thumb and forefinger, it tricks your body into thinking your left hand is in a good position,which it is not. The thumb feels good,but the rest of your left hand is in a weak (turned to far left) position. From here, the club face will be open at impact, robbing you of power and producing a weak slice that will have you looking in the right rough or woods all day. Again, not a very rewarding ball flight. If you have difficulty closing the gap, slide your left thumb up the grip towards your wrist, this is called a short thumb. Many good players do this to ensure that all of the left hand is on the club correctly (Figure 4.3)

GRIP FAULT NUMBER 4 =GRIPPING TOO TIGHTLY. This is a golf club, not a sledgehammer. We want to swish the golf ball way out there, not hurt it. Did you know that your grip pressure sets the tension level of your swing? Watch any good player and you will see soft hands. When our grip pressure is too tight, the tension starts in our hands, goes right up our arms and straight

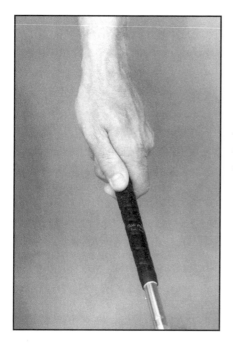

Figure 4.3. Close the gap next to the thumb for even more control.

across our chest. Next thing you know, we are stiff as a board and chopping, not smoothly swinging with confidence. It's a good idea to have a grip pressure thought. Use any thought you like; holding a bird, an open tube of toothpaste, a banana. I know this for sure; I personally can't expect to hit my best shot if my hands are too tight. So my final action in a pressure situation is to take a slow, deep breath, relax my hands, and let it fly. We hear this advice all of our golfing career, yet it is one of the hardest things to accomplish. Many tight grips are the result of holding the club incorrectly. We get no zip to our swing if our hands are too tight. Soften up your hands, relax your wrists, and hear some swish when you swing.

GRIP FAULT NUMBER 5 = NOT HAVING THE LIFE LINE OF YOUR RIGHT HAND COVERING YOUR LEFT THUMB. I see a lot of interesting combinations here. We need to form a soft, solid assembly by getting the palm pocket where the life line is on your right palm over and covering your left thumb. It should fit nicely. If it doesn't, you are either gripping too tightly or holding the club too much in the right palm, not in the fingers where it should be. A common mistake I see here is the right hand turned too far under the grip. We should not be able to see the left thumb or much of the fingernails on the right hand. When this does occur, we have the tendency to pull the club to the inside on the take away. The can lead to an over-the-top move, hitting the ground hard, and even the dreaded hosel shot. So let's get that grip right.

Most of us learned to get our grip with the club on the ground. I believe this adds to the probability of these faults occurring while we're bent over fumbling with our club. The ground can turn the club, it can ride up in the crease of our palm, not to mention it stresses our back. After years of watching this happen, I am convinced most of these problems can be eliminated by getting your grip with the club in the air, out in front of you. We can seat the club correctly, square the blade easily, and save our back for more important things. Let's go through getting our grip together. There is no easy way to describe how to get a good grip. I have taken the liberty of using lots of pictures, so you can see how a good grip looks. Take your time with each step. If it feels odd to you when you get your new grip, that's good, it means that you have changed something. If it feels the same, nothing changed. Remember at first, if it feels good, it's probably wrong. Let's go step by step.

If you play left handed, simply reverse these instructions.

Step 1. Take a 7 or 8 iron and hold it with your right hand just below the grip. Holding the club parallel with the ground out in front of you, place the grip in your left hand where the fingers meet the hand. (Figure 4.4) Now softly wrap the rest of your hand over the top of the grip until we can see two knuckles on the back of

your left hand. Grip down ¼"
from the butt end of the club,
and make sure the gap between
the thumb and forefinger is
closed. Look at the lines on the
club face. If they are not
straight up and down (perpendicular to the ground), adjust
the club now by loosening your
grip and moving the club until
the lines on the club face are
straight up and down (Figure
4.5). When they are, you have
a square club. If they are angled
to the left (Figure 4.6), the club

Figure 4.4. Hold your club out in front of you to ensure you grip it correctly, with the club laying across the line where your fingers and hand meet.

face is closed. If the lines are angled to the right (Figure 4.7) the
club face is open. This is your only reference to square on the golf
course. This is going to be very important during the pre-shot routine we use on the course. So now our left hand should be seated
below the palm pad and ready to go (Figure 4.8).

Step 2. Now we need to put the right hand on. There are three
acceptable choices we can make with the pinky or little finger of
our right hand. The Vardon or overlap grip is one that overlaps the
right pinkie finger in the notch formed by the left forefinger and
second finger. This grip method is used by most good players because it keeps your hands soft while at the same time giving you a
solid grip assembly.

The second option is the interlocking grip where your right
hand pinkie interlocks with the left hand forefinger. This should be
used by golfers with small or weak hands. Many seniors that I teach

Figure 4.5. If the lines on the club face are straight up and down (perpendicular), the blade is square.

Figure 4.6. A blade angled to the left is considered closed.

Figure 4.7. A blade angled to the right is considered open.

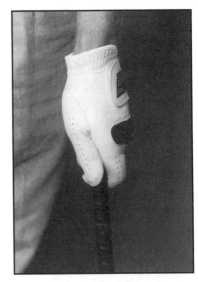

Figure 4.8. This is what a good left hand grip looks like.

use this grip without realizing this last option; the ten-finger grip. This is when all ten fingers are on the club. The pinkie neither overlaps or interlocks. You should try this, at least for a while. You may like it. The ten-finger grip allows you to hold the club firmly, yet not too tight. It promotes good use of the wrists and forearms for anyone who has historically been too stiff. Lastly, if you have any arthritis, it simply gives you a better grip and more control.

Choose a grip that fits your needs, and, as with all the principles we discuss, don't be afraid to experiment. Whatever right hand grip you go with, this next step is important to get right. As we put our right hand on the club, place it across the second notch in the fingers. (Figure 4.9). Now softly bring your hand over the top, making sure you cover the left thumb with the pocket on the right hand where the life line is. We now have a neutral grip. If we were to open our hands as they grip the club and extend our fingers, you will notice our fingers point straight down at the ground (Figure 4.10). This is how our body is built and where our hands want to release naturally at impact. This is what good players count on. This is also how good players can work the ball by making small subtle changes in their grip. Notice in any of the set-up pictures throughout the book that both v's formed by the thumbs and forefingers on both hands point at my right eye. Check your grip and see if it looks the same. If yours looks a bit sloppy, milk your hands toward the center line of the golf club, that is to turn your left hand slightly to the right, and your right hand slightly to the left. You will feel your arms extend when you do this.

Since the grip is so important, I ask my students to practice it as much as they can. A good way to do this is when you are watching television. Have a club handy, and every time a commercial comes on, get your grip and square the blade while you are still

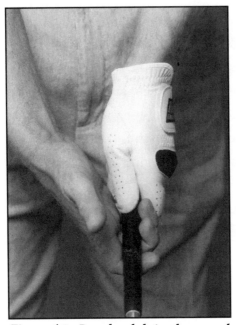

Figure 4.9. Put the club in the second notch in the right fingers to ensure a solid grip assembly.

sitting down. This way you will become more comfortable getting your grip with the club in the air, instead of standing up and grounding the club. Who needs to watch all those crazy commercials anyway? If you are eating buttered popcorn, watch that butter on the grip. This could lead to a severe loss of control on the course, plus you would have to lick your fingers after each swing.

The grip is one of the most underestimated parts of a good swing. It takes practice and patience, a "feel" if you will. I always warn my students that it's one of the hardest things to change; any grip change is extremely uncomfortable at first. There is one shortcut that I know of that will help you out if you are struggling with your grip. It's called a grip trainer. A molded

Figure 4.10. If you have a neutral grip, and open your hands, your fingers will point straight down. This is how your body is built.

rubber grip is installed on one of your clubs, and when you put your hands on the club, they are in the correct position. These grips can be purchased at any golf shop and are wonderful for training your hands how to grip the club correctly. They are not for everyday play, as that gives you an unfair advantage over others, but they will reinforce the feel of a good grip. So if you hang in there, stick with it and practice, it will be well worth it as you set the first foundation to a great senior swing, the grip.

STANCE AND BALANCE

We now have a solid grip and need to address our next senior fundamentals, stance and balance. I would like to clear up something in the balance department right away. It's that misunderstood notion that your weight should be on your heels when you are addressing the ball. Think about it for a moment. Is there any athletic sport that you do from your heels? The answer is clearly no, yet I hear people all the time trying to help their friends by saying, "It should feel like you're sitting on a barstool." Whoever thought that one up must have been sitting on a barstool too long! All moving sports have something in common. It's called dynamic balance and it means a moving balance. All these moving sports have something else in common. The balance point is on the balls of our feet, not our heels. Imagine what would happen if you played tennis on your heels. Or how about we go dancing and put our weight firmly on our heels? It wouldn't work, would it? Senior golfers especially need to balance on the balls of the feet. By doing so, it allows us to use all of our body instead of only our arms, we can generate more club head speed, and follow through more easily. An added bonus is it will take a tremendous amount of stress off your back.

To feel the correct spot for your weight to be, try these balance drills that I do with my students. Get your grip, then place the club on your shoulder like you are going to hit a baseball. Sense where your weight is. It should be on the balls of your feet and you should feel springy (Figure 4.11). Now place the club head on the ground behind the ball and maintain that balance. Another good thought is to make sure you could dance from your setup balance point. That will get you into balance, so let's add that to our setup.

Figure 4.11. The balance used in golf is the same as many other sports, including baseball. Your weight should be on the balls of your feet.

When we are balanced correctly, we have more bend at our waist than in our knees (Figure 4.12). Take a peek in a mirror and make sure this is how you are setting up. If you have too much knee flex, you will feel out of balance. Also, if you have too much flex in your knees, ist's almost impossible to stay level during your swing. I call it a topped shot waiting to happen.

I believe your body has a natural swinging height, but if you have too much knee flex it throws this natural height off. You start your back swing, but your knees and back are so stressed that your body stands up to protect itself. Now you are at a different height than when you started and the trouble is about to begin. Since your brain picks up the fact that you have changed your height, it's going to send messages to your muscles to dip on the downswing to counteract standing up on the back swing. There are only three things that can happen from here. You can: 1. Get lucky with

Figure 4.12. There is more bend at the waist than at the knees when we are balanced correctly.

your timing and catch it well, 2. Mistime it and hit the ground heavy, or 3. Mistime it and catch it thin by hitting the top half of the ball. We want to take luck out of the equation, so let's get the proper knee flex for our natural height, and get rid of an area that sounds insignificant but can cause a lot of trouble.

A question that I am asked frequently is how far from the ball should we be standing? With the sole of the club resting flat on the ground, the butt end of the grip should be one hand width away from our body when we are balanced at address (Figure 4.13). This is a good general measurement to use for all clubs. The longer the club, the farther we will stand away from the ball, but we will always be one sideways hand away from the butt of the club. If we

Figure 4.13. The butt end of the grip should be about one hand width away from out left leg at address.

are too far from the ball, the toe of the club will be sticking slightly up in the air, not flat on the ground as it should be. A set up that is too far from the ball will cause us to take the club too much around the back of us, otherwise known as a flat swing. This will result in a lot of topped shots, and put strain on our lower back. Standing too far from the ball is much more common than standing too close. Standing too close would be kind of obvious, because you would hit the ground on the downswing. Most people will only do this a few times before they make the correct adjustment and stand slightly farther away from the club. So while you are checking your set up in the mirror, make sure you are a hand width away with your arms hanging naturally. Another small thing that makes a big difference.

YOUR LEFT FOOT

Think back to when you started golfing. If you are like me, you were probably told to put your feet square to the target line.

Here again is something I see senior golfers struggle with time and time again, with frustrating consequences. It usually starts with a new student whom I have never seen hit a ball say, "Jim, I always hit the ball to the right because I can't follow through. When I look at their setup, their feet are at 90° angles to the target line. The student's reaction is always the same, "I thought my feet were supposed to be square to the target line?" As senior golfers, our flexibility has changed and keeping our feet square to the target line will not do. Our feet should be on line with the target, but we need to flare them out to be able to move through the shot.

It used to be that by keeping your feet square, you would have to go to a reverse-c position on your follow through. Then they discovered that the reverse-c would wreck your back. This is also why golf was so hard to learn years ago. The only way you could learn this "classic swing" is if you were either made out of rubber or you didn't mind hobbling home after a round to soak your aching back.

How much should we flare our feet out? The left foot will be flared out more than the right, and your flexibility level will dictate the amount you flare it out. Anywhere from 20° to 45° is perfectly acceptable for seniors. If straight ahead is 12 o'clock, then you want your left foot flared between 10 and 11 o'clock. Later in this chapter we will do a pistol drill to learn the correct way to follow through. At that point we will experiment with what is the correct amount of flair for you. Remember that everyone has different levels of flexibility, so there is no correct amount of flair to your feet as long as you feel comfortable, it's at least 11 o'clock, and you can follow through.

TOE UP TO TOE UP

This next area is where, as seniors, we will be able to generate more speed and power, while learning to hit it straighter. It's called toe to toe and it describes the correct club head rotation, which is the motion foundation of all golf swings. My senior students always enjoy learning this particular theory because the results are often dramatic. Let's first back up a bit. As I was learning the golf swing, all I ever heard was "body turn, body turn, body turn." I guess everyone assumed that I knew how to use my hands, but I had no clue. I still never hear much about the hand, wrist, and forearm function in the swing. I feel this is especially important for senior golfers. Please don't misunderstand what I am saying, it is very important to use your body turn in the golf swing. The primary source of power for the golf swing is the shoulders turning 90° and the hips turning 45° during the swing.

The problem is that many golfers get so hung up on body turn that they forget the other part. We need to get speed and power from anywhere it's available, and this is a source of speed just waiting to be used. The hands, wrists, and forearms create the second lever in a true two-lever golf swing, and are severely underestimated as an additional source of power by most golfers. If you are missing this second lever, you obviously would only have a one-lever swing. If it feels like you are shoveling the ball down the fairway like a giant putt, not creating any swish in your swing, and wearing yourself out in the process, you may be missing this lever. Let's explore how we can generate more speed by inviting the hands, wrists, and forearms to join in on the fun. As we add this second lever, we will create centrifugal force, which is one of the major forces in the swing. Let's see what this toe up to toe up is and how it can help us.

The object of our swing is to swing our club square to the swing plane, or path, the club takes throughout the swing. Many golfers think that means taking the club straight back and straight through. That would work fine if we were using a croquet mallet, where the shaft goes into the center and we didn't need to rotate it. But this is a golf club, and the shaft goes into the rear of the club, making it necessary for us to rotate the club to keep it square to the swing plane and to generate more force.

If the club is not square to the swing plane throughout the swing, it will be out of balance and not working effectively. For the club to swing square to the swing plane, it should move in a toe up to toe up fashion. What does that mean? When the club is at nine o'clock and three o 'clock, parallel to the ground, the toe of the club must be pointing at the sky. The foundation to our golf swing is as simple as that, toe up to toe up.

If we go through these two positions, once on our back swing, and once on our follow through, the rest of our swing motion will occur naturally. Our wrists will hinge correctly and our swing will sequence the way it should, with little extra effort. Once we go through these two positions, the rest of your swing will occur according to your strength and level of flexibility. How am I accomplishing this? Notice in the sequence (Figure 4.14.1 and Figure 4.14.2), you can see the face of my watch on the back swing and the clasp of my watch on the forward swing. Face of the watch, clasp of the watch. Face then clasp, toe-up to toe-up and so on. When the club is in a toe-up position at nine o'clock in the back swing it is square to the swing plane. When I swish it through to a toe-up position at three o'clock, it is still square to the swing plane, but it has released. You may have heard of that term before. Releasing the club is simply both levers unloading their power at the same time;

Figure 4.14.1. See the face of the watch, then the clasp? This is toe up to toe up, the basic foundation of club head rotation.

right at impact. Now here is the question of the day. If at nine o'clock the club is square to the swing plane (toe up), and at three o'clock the club is also square to the swing plane (toe up again), where do you think the club will be at impact? If you said square, give yourself two attaboys, (or attagirls), the golf clap, and a pat on the back because you're right.

To learn this feel, let's swish our club back and forth, toe up to toe up, so we can generate speed, feel release, and hit it straight. It should feel soft and relaxed, smooth and balanced. This is a great exercise to do at home to get the feel of toe up to toe up. You don't even have to hit balls, you can just swish the club back and forth. Occasionally, I encounter students that have too tight a grip to feel the proper swishing motion. If you still feel stiff, try this drill. Separate your hands about 1" on your grip. Now lightly swish the club back and forth, toe up to toe up. Feel how your wrists snap as the club travels through impact? That is release. Remember, splitting

Figure 4.14.2

your grip is only a drill, so don't hit balls or swing hard using this drill.

Now onto my favorite drill. It's the feet together toe up to toe up drill. Put a ball on a short tee and grab your seven iron. With your feet about four or five inches apart at the heels, flare out your left foot and get balanced on the balls of your feet. Now simply go toe up to toe up, three o'clock to nine o'clock and hit it. It may take you a few balls to get it down, but once you do, wow, it should feel good.

Remember, this is not a distance test, simply a drill designed to teach us how to use our hands, wrists, and forearms correctly. We should feel what it's like to hit ball after ball straight, and understand the role the second lever plays in our swing. As you become more comfortable with hitting the ball, extend the back swing and follow through slightly. Don't swing too hard, because we have not gotten to a follow through yet. When we add a follow through to this, we will experience straighter shots, more club head speed, release, centrifugal force, and all the benefits of an effortless two-lever swing. Before we go on to the follow through we need to address the vision problems that many of us have which affect our swing greatly but are often overlooked.

BIFOCAL BACKSWING; SHORTER IS BETTER

I have been wearing glasses since I was a child. In many of the things I do, I must make adjustments. I have studied this with my students for years and feel that wearing glasses affects the golf swing more profoundly than in other sports. If you wear glasses, as many seniors do, the adjustments you make can mean the difference between playing the game effectively or struggling to do something you are not capable of doing. I will explain why you need to shorten your back swing to hit the ball effectively. I call this shortened back swing that helps glasses wearers play more effectively the "Bifocal Backswing," and whether you wear glasses or not, you will find it most interesting. I'll explain.

We know ideally our chin should be up at address so that our shoulders move freely under our chin during the back swing and we don't slouch. This also helps us create a spine angle of around 30°, which gives us a solid center to swing around. The problem is that if we get into this so called "perfect position" with our chin up, and we wear any type of glasses, we are either looking through the reading part of our bifocals, or looking through the bottom rim of our glasses. This can distort our depth perception and our ability to see the ball clearly. The adjustment that I see almost all golfers who wear glasses make is to lower their chin into or close to their chest. This way, they are looking through the middle of their glasses and have a relatively clear view of that pretty little ball just sitting there waiting to be whacked.

The real problem occurs when they start their back swing. As the shoulders turn, the chin, which is buried into the chest, is swept away. This often produces a sway that is all but impossible to recover from. It's now almost as if you are trying to hit a moving target. You may get lucky now and again and make solid contact, however there is another added aspect of timing to the swing that you don't want. Surely golf is hard enough already.

In many of the early golf lessons I took, I was told, "c'mon, turn back farther, you can do it," as if there were something wrong with me because I couldn't seem to get the club back to parallel. The harder I tried to take it way back, the worse I got, until I almost quit. It took me a while, but I finally figured out it was a vision problem, not a lack of talent. I developed a set up and back swing that work well. When it comes to teaching my senior students, many of whom wear glasses, they find it much easier to make solid contact with the Bifocal Backswing, a shorter back swing that allows us glasses wearers to go back far enough to generate power, but not far enough for our glasses to hinder our ability to make solid contact. For you senior golfers who don't wear glasses, this section is still worth learning. Most senior golfers could benefit from a more compact back swing, and the results may surprise you. Remember, the object is to give you an efficient golf swing that is powerful and repeatable. The bottom line is that it is easier to shorten your back swing, than to try to time a long, looping, ineffective swing. Read on.

If you wear bifocals, get a pair of single vision glasses to play golf in, and throw a cheap pair of reading glasses in your bag to keep score with. If you can't afford this, then we can make your bifocals work, you will just have to be extra careful on how far back you swing. Next, we need to check our set up. Grab your trusty 7 or 6 iron and get into an address position standing sideways to a mirror. Is your chin buried in your chest? If so, raise your chin as high as you can and still be able to clearly see the ball. Any extra space we can get between the chin and the chest will be an improvement.

Now start the Bifocal Backswing. Whether you wear glasses or not, the objective is to take the club back as far as you can and still meet these criteria;

1. The shoulders don't move the head more than 1" off the ball.
2. The soft extension in the left (or lead) arm, and good 90° wrist hinge are retained.
3. You are relaxed and in balance.
4. You can see the ball.

We need to get that antiquated theory, "If you don't get the club back to parallel, you're no good," out of our minds. With our Bifocal Backswing we will not only generate plenty of swing speed, but we will never sacrifice centeredness of hit again. I like to explain it to my students like this; suppose you were going to hammer in a nail to hang a picture. Would you take the hammer so far back that it would be behind your back? Of course not. What do you think you would hit? Chances are you would get the nail once in a while, but you would also blast your fingers, the wall, and anything else that happened to get in the way. You would have lost control by trying to go back farther than you need to. Sound familiar?

We need a much higher level of precision in golf, and we need controlled acceleration. Not unlike swinging a hammer, an overswing can cause a severe loss of control, but that's not all. When we overswing our grip can come apart too. As we know, if our grip falls apart we have an extra moving part that has to reset itself on the down swing. The swing is hard enough without another moving part. A simple test is to put a dime on your left thumb (Figure 4.15) and cover it with your right palm. Now take your back swing and if the dime comes out, you are pushing your back swing too far back.

Repeat this test until you can do it without your dime slipping while you retain soft extension in your left arm. Another by-product of an over swing is the possibility of your shoulders springing first on the down swing. This creates an overly steep swing and you can hit the ground pretty hard. This steep swing, by the way, can be one of the reasons you have those ugly scratch marks on the top of your new driver. We will talk

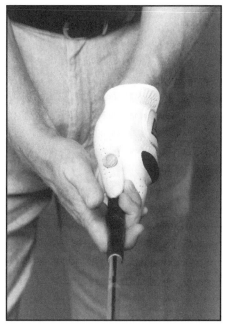

Figure 4.15. Put a dime in your grip to find out if it falls apart during your swing.

about that part a little more in the following chapters.

So let's get back to the four criteria for the Bifocal Backswing.

1. If the shoulders move the head more than an inch off the ball going back, you have started to sway. If you sway going back, then you have to sway the same amount on your forward swing to even have a chance of hitting it crisply. As you can imagine, this makes the entire swing much more difficult to time. Try this simple test. Get your set-up position in front of a mirror. Make a mark on the mirror with lipstick or a crayon where the bridge of your nose is at set up . Take your normal back swing and see how far you moved. If you went much more than an inch, then you are swaying, not turning. Practice in slow motion until you can stay steady by turning. Shorten your back swing if you need to.

2.Our left (or lead) arm need not be rigid. This is another old swing theory that does not hold true today. Yes, the arm should be extended, but it should also be tension free. Imagine a whip that was stiff as a board. Could you get enough speed to crack it? I should say not, yet I see golfers all the time trying to achieve maximum extension by keeping their lead arm stiff as a steel rod. The results can be disastrous. Keep those arms soft, yet extended, and create a 90° angle at the wrists. The maintaining of this angle is a fabulous source of power, and much easier to accomplish with a shorter back swing. By the way, a side benefit of getting your grip with the club in the air is that your arm will extend naturally and you really don't have to think about it.

3. You will be relaxed and in balance during your Bifocal Backswing. Often when students of mine start to shorten up their back swing, they somehow feel that they must make up for not going back as far by swinging like a maniac. I assure you this is not necessary, we will more than make up for it with crisp contact, a stronger follow through, and a strong compact motion verses a wild glancing blow. Take it back where you still feel balanced and in control.

4. You will have your chin up as high as you can and you'll still see the ball.

Your Bifocal Backswing will probably be considerably shorter than it was in the past. That is completely acceptable. Everyone has a different level of flexibility, so everyone's back swing length will vary. You don't need to go back a mile to hit a good shot, glasses or not. My back swing is to about ten o'clock with my left arm, yet is very effective. By practicing this Bifocal Backswing, your ball striking should become much more consistent. The better you get at contacting the center of the club face, the more solid your shots will feel and the farther they will go.

A great way to test the effectiveness of your back swing is this. Take your club back and hold your back swing for five seconds. If it feels comfortable and not strained, and it meets the four criteria of the Bifocal Backswing, then it is a back swing that will work for you. Now to complete our swing with a beautiful follow through.

A FOLLOW THROUGH YOU CAN DO

To me, one of the most rewarding aspects of teaching is when you enlighten someone who was sure that they could not do something. With my senior students, follow through has to be the most popular candidate in the "I can't do that" department. Yet it never ceases to amaze those same students just how easy it is to get a beautiful follow through. First of all, what does a follow through do and why do we need it? Among other things, a follow through has three main functions:

1. It allows the club to continue down the target line. If you are cutting off your follow through early, the club more than likely is making a hard left turn around your body at the end of the swing. If you release the club at impact, your shot will probably go low and left. If you hold onto it (don't release) it, the likely shot pattern is starting left and slicing right, sometimes you will get lucky again, but once we follow through we can continue the club down the target line.

2. A follow through is an outlet for club head speed. Think of it this way. If your follow through is not completed, chances are the fastest part of your swing was not at impact either. It is critical, especially since we are shortening our back swing, that we follow through so there is somewhere for all that whoosh to go. I have always been a firm believer in a forward, swing-oriented swing mo-

tion. We hit the ball swinging forward anyway. This next scenario may describe you. You take a monumental back swing only to have it run out of steam at impact. This means your back swing is longer than your forward swing. This is also the recipe for deceleration and disaster. We need to invert that swing. Make the follow through longer than the back swing. This will create an accelerating swing. That's a lot better!

3. A good follow through prevents injury. If you look at the pistol drill sequence on this page, you will notice that my trunk and spine rotate together, taking an awful lot of stress off my back. If you don't follow through correctly, your upper body twists all the way around while your lower body lags behind. This move creates tremendous stress on your back. A good follow through also takes much of the stress off your right shoulder. Again, if your lower body doesn't keep up with your upper body, the force of the club moving past impact will yank on your right shoulder every time you swing. Lastly, our knees are affected by our follow through. A good follow through has the left leg fully extended, not bent and moving laterally which can cause injury. Since we should not be hurting ourselves golfing, the only logical answer is to learn to follow through, so let's get to it.

There are three things we look for when our follow through is complete.

1. The hands are up next to the left ear.

2. The belt buckle is facing the target.

3. The right toe is pointing into the ground, with the majority of the weight on the left foot.

How can we accomplish this? With my favorite follow through drill, the pistol drill. We need to teach our feet what they are supposed to be doing. Our arms know what they are doing from the

Figure 4.16.1. The pistol drill will teach you the body motion required to have an effortless follow through.

toe up to toe up drill. They already want to go up to the left ear. And certainly the belt buckle wants to turn toward the target. So this should be easier than you think. Stand erect, flare out your left foot and put your right elbow on your side. Now make a pistol with your fingers in your right hand. Now turn and shoot the target.(Figure 4.16.1 and Figure 4.16.2). When you are done, you should be able to

hold your balance, almost all of your weight should be on your left foot, and you should be standing erect with your left leg straight. Don't be afraid to roll out on the side of your left foot. Practice this drill, and add it to the toe up to toe up drill. This will give you a balanced swing that is controlled, powerful, effortless, and finishes with a follow through that is as effective as it is beautiful.

Figure 4.16.2.

Once you start to follow through on all of your full swings, an amazing thing happens. You begin to set your own personal swing speed, a swing speed that works best for you and lets you maintain control of the club, while still achieving maximum velocity. You will start to realize that any swing that you don't follow through was not your best chance at a good shot. In fact, if you don't get to your follow through position, you will feel awkward, as if you forgot part of your swing. A good follow through will get you out of the crush mode, and into the swing mode. I enjoy watching students make the transition from a short, choppy swing to a smooth swing with a follow through. Since many of us have played sports our whole lives, we tend to put too much strength effort into golf. It is especially a problem if we are learning the game as adults, when our strength level far exceeds our golfing experience level. That usually leaves us one choice, kill the ball. Once we start to follow through, we realize that smoothness counts. We also realize that golf has more in common with ballet and fly casting than hockey and football. You can't swing hard enough to be out of control and still have a good follow through. Get to a smooth follow through on all of your full swings and watch your tempo become perfect.

TO SUM IT UP

So let's review this chapter and get a reasonable plan of attack to implement the things that we've learned. We need a good grip, that's number one. We could have all the other parts down perfect, but if our grip assembly is bad we're not going anywhere. Practice your grip at home, sitting down. When we have a sound grip assembly, check your balance and posture in a mirror. Go outside and swish the club through the toe to toe up points. If you feel stiff, split your grip and try it some more. Do your pistol drill to promote a good follow through whenever you can. When you have turned these drills into repeatable feelings, it's off to the range to try some of it. Start off by warming up, of course, then use the toe up drill first. Feet 4"-5"apart at the heels, left foot flared, weight on the balls of your feet, relaxed and comfortable. Go toe up to toe up, nine o'clock to three o'clock and hit some smooth shots off a tee, not for distance, but for smoothness. When you have the ball going straight effortlessly, start to lengthen your swing to a follow through. This is an important time to remember your Bifocal Backswing and not to start over-swinging. Practice, practice, and then practice some more. This will result in a flowing swing motion that will give you straighter, longer shots. I believe that anyone can get better, so check all the components of your swing and have fun. Now we will take each club group individually and see how each works.

CHAPTER **5**

The Full Swing
Using the Different Clubs

I n the last chapter we built the foundation of our swing
motion. Now it's time to start working on the different
club groups. Golfers often ask me if we use the same
swing motion for all the clubs in our bag. The answer is yes. Except
for minor set up differences, we use the same basic swing motion
for all of the clubs in our bag when we take a full swing. So why do
I break it down into club groups? Every student I teach has different needs. One student may be having difficulty driving the ball off
the tee, whereas another will be struggling with their mid and short
irons. Even though we do use the same basic swing motion, the
subtle changes in each club's set up at address makes all the difference in how effectively you will hit any given shot. The previous
chapter will straighten out your swing motion, and this chapter will
isolate all the different clubs for you to work on them one group at
a time. Feel free to check all your club groups with the hints and
instruction in this chapter. If you have particular problems with
one group, concentrate your efforts there first.

DRIVING THE BALL

Teaching seniors to drive the ball better is one of my favorite subjects. I know the old adage "drive for show, putt for dough" is true, but there is an undeniable thrill we all feel when we nail our tee shot and look up to see our ball seeking the center of the fairway. Did you ever notice how a great tee shot commands instant respect from all who witness it? Let's make no mistake about it, your tee shot sets the tone for the hole. No worse tone can be set than by topping your tee shot, hitting behind it, popping it up, or hitting it sideways into the one place you didn't want to. To start this chapter off we will learn to hit our drives straight and far. It sounds like an impossible task, but it's really not that hard.

We have discussed the proper club rotation, toe-up to toe-up in the preceding chapters. This also applies to the woods. One of the fastest ways to slice a wood is not to release the club to a toe-up position as we go through the shot. The reason this occurs with amateurs so often is because their grip is way too tight to allow the release to occur, and they swing too hard. Is this the fault of the golfer? Of course not. The club itself tries to make you do this. It's long, it's got a big head, but most important it is whispering to you on the tee "I'll bet you could hit me 250 yards if you really take a mighty swing at it." So time and time again your body obliges and starts preparing itself on the tee box. Everyone is looking, but you know this is going to be good, you can sense it. As you begin to settle in over your shot, you take one last look at the pin 360 yards away (instead of the fairway 220 yards away). Back goes the club. Turn as far as you can to get distance. Now,unbeknownst to you, your hands are holding on for dear life and have effectively turned your golf club into a sledge hammer. Down we go to the ball, it's all a blur, it's going on so fast. Our body, knowing that we will hurt ourselves if we continue at this breakneck swing speed, protects us by abandoning the follow through, making us fall away at the end of our swing. We are rewarded with a glancing blow that goes at best high right and has only half of the distance we think we deserve according to the amount of effort we put into the shot. It's all right, we tell ourselves, it will get better next time, but it never seems to get under control.

We first need to understand our weapon of choice, this driver in our bag. It can deliver a perfect, effortless tee shot that arcs down the middle, making us the envy and gaining the respect of all who watch. Only minutes later it can reduce us to embarrassment and frustration by dribbling 30 feet into the pond in front of the tee. I don't know of a better feeling shot than when your drive is pure. Conversely, nothing seems to be able to get you into more trouble than a tee shot gone awry.

Why so much variety in the shots it can produce? First of all the driver has the least amount of loft of any club in the bag (except the putter of course). Remember this basic premise for all of your clubs, loft produces back spin which counteracts or negates side spin. Since our pal side spin is responsible for hooks and slices, and a driver does not have enough loft to overcome side spin, it's easier to find trouble with a slice or hook. Secondly, the driver in your bag is probably between 43" and 46" long, making it hard to control due to its length. Thirdly, with the intentions of hitting the ball into the next zip code, we have the tendency to swing just a little hard at it every once in a while. This hard swing tightens the hands and you know what happens from there: "FORE RIGHT" or even worse: " #%$¢&¢%**¢#$#%."

We should put our driver into perspective before we learn more about using it correctly. The players on the professional tours hit the fairway around 70% to 80% of the time. We should expect to hit the fairway about 60% of the time, which would be great, wouldn't it? That's six out of 10 times, folks. As senior golfers get better, we can increase that percentage depending on how far we hit it. Remember, the farther you hit it, the more likely you are to hit it off line. If you don't hit your tee shots more than 180 yards, you should make up for length with accuracy and expect to hit a higher percentage of fairways. Also the driver is what I call an area club. I would love to tell you that you should be able to hit it onto a tablecloth in the fairway, but that's not very realistic. Remember this phrase when you have your driver in hand, "if I can find it, I can hit it again." I give myself a very broad target when I use my driver, and you should too! If there is any doubt in my mind that I may miss my intended area, I have the wrong club in my hand. We will discuss that in more detail in the course management section, later in this book.

Driving the ball well is a progressive skill. Rest assured, I did not learn to hit a seven iron solidly, then pick up a driver and start striping it down the middle. Rule number one is this: you must learn to use a more lofted wood effectively first, then it will be easier to learn to use the driver. A student will call me and ask for a driver lesson. We loosen up and then I will ask him to hit a few five woods off the tee. If he can't hit a five wood off the tee, no sense trying a driver. A five wood typically has 22° loft, which is two times the loft on most drivers, effectively making it twice as easy to hit. I have my students learn the five wood first. When you can hit seven out of 10 comfortably in play, then it's time to go to the three wood. It usually has 16° loft and is ½ again easier to hit than the driver. Because of its loft, it goes just slightly shorter than a driver, but goes much farther than a five wood. Many students shake off the lure of 10 more yards by forgetting their driver and sticking with the three wood. Since so much more consistency can be gained with a three wood, many golfers find themselves playing from the middle of the fairway after they leave their drivers in the closet. This is a decision you alone have to make, however here is a good tip for you to help in your decision. Try to find the catagory that applies to you and use the suggestion that follows.

A) If you hit your average tee shot under 150 yards, try a driver with an A or L flex shaft, 11°, 12°, or 13° loft. This should help you get more distance and the added loft will still help get it airborne.

B) If you hit your normal tee shot 190 yards, a three wood in R flex would work well for your every day driving. You could put an 11° A or R flex driver in your bag for wide open holes, but self control would be needed not to pull it out at the wrong time.

C) If you drive the ball 220 yards or more, then a 10° or 11° in a strong R shaft would work, but your three wood should still be your bread and butter driving club.

D) If you are a single-digit handicap, you already know the value of being in the middle of the fairway, that's why you have a single-digit handicap.

Many years ago when I was a young professional, my wife and I would drive her grandparents to Florida just after Christmas each year. Debbie's aunt, knowing I would be looking for someone to play with, set up some games with her boss, a very good player. I never knew what driving the ball straight meant until I watched this man play. Of course, in Florida if you hit it off line, it's in the jungle where there are things waiting to eat you. Anyway, after three days of seeing him hit almost every fairway, I asked him if I could see his driver. He said he would be happy to show it to me if he had one, but he just used the three wood for control. That's when I learned that it's not how far you hit it, but it's how far you hit it under control.

How about these driving irons we hear so much about? They are pretty much 1, 2, and 3 irons with larger, hollow heads. They look like irons and swing very similar to woods. Some of my students swear by them, and some swear at them. I like to see you use woods because they are more versatile, but I don't think you can hurt yourself if you try a demo driving iron along the way.

I like to think of driving as tempo and timing. Tempo because most golfers swing too fast and timing because you must release the club at precisely the correct instant or hit a less than perfect shot. If you look at an eight iron and a driver, what is the difference? Loft, length, and the size of the head. Let's focus on the length since we already know how loft can effect our shot.

When you swing an eight iron, it will make a certain size circle or swing arc. A driver is going to make a much larger swing arc because the club is so much longer. Making a larger arc, it will take more time to get back to the ball, so we don't want to rush it. We must let the club do its job without our interference. I like using this example for my students. Think of how you use a small hammer, and how you use a larger one. Even though they both do the same job, the larger hammer has a few subtle differences. It creates more force with a longer, slower stroke. It is the same basic function, just slower and smoother. When I put a larger hammer in my hands, I don't grit my teeth and swing furiously until I lose control. This is how we must think of our driver, just another club, except we will have to wait for it to finish the back swing before we swing down. Now if this club is going to take longer to get back to the ball, wouldn't it make sense to keep your eyes focused on the ball a while longer? Of course it would, yet we all are guilty of coming up out of our shot early once in a while. By doing so, we open our shoulders early and don't let the club swing down and through, which can cause quite the banana. So two of my favorite basics for driving the ball well are to take your time to let the club swing without forcing it, and keeping your eyes on it a split second longer to let the club continue down the target line. Notice in (Figure 5.1) my club is past the ball, but I still am looking at the spot where the

Figure 5.1. My ball is gone, but I'm still looking at the spot where the ball was.

ball was, in effect staying into the shot longer. From here we can just let centrifugal force take over and pull us up out of the shot to a follow through. What's that you say, you're not generating any centrifugal force? We can correct that, too!

Remember as seniors we need to generate club head speed any way we can. One of the quickest ways to get more speed in your swing is to learn to release the club. This adds speed instantly and ends the powerless swing that you work too hard for. A favorite drill of mine is the split grip drill to help my students feel what this release is all about. We used this drill to relax tight hands, but it is also a wonderful drill to feel the timing and release of your driver swing.

Take your driver and get your grip, but separate your hands about 1" apart on the club (Figure 5.2). Simply swing the club gently back and forth, paying particular attention to what your arms,

Figure 5.2. Take a wood, separate your grip 1", and swing it easily to feel the release at impact.

wrists, and hands are doing. This is a function of release. Please don't swing hard, hit the ground, or hit balls with this drill. It is designed to teach you a feeling. You will feel centrifugal force and pendulum motion. You should also feel a little snap at impact. This is what good players feel. If we go back (Figure 5.1), notice how my right hand has rolled over my left after impact. If this does not occur during your swing, you are steering the ball and only getting half of the swing speed that you deserve. Can you overrotate the hands in the swing? Yes, you can. Like every other part of the golf swing, release can be exaggerated to the point of not being beneficial any more. As seniors, we want to take advantage of the release, but your body must move in conjunction with your arms. Make sure when you do the split grip drill that you are following through. If you are not, go back to the pistol drill until your body is moving to a follow through and then do the split grip drill. This will prepare us to learn how to drive it deeply.

To hit a great tee shot, it's important to get our set up correct. The ball position should coincide with your tee height. When hitting a wood off a tee, one half of the ball should be above the top of the club face. Today's jumbo woods have a much deeper face, yet I observe many golfers with the ball teed up way too low to satisfy this rule of thumb. When the ball is teed too low, we have a tendency to come in too steep after it and pop the ball up. With a standard size driver head, tee it up with half of the ball above the top of the club, and play it off the instep of your left foot. If you have a jumbo head on your driver, tee it up slightly higher and play it more forward toward your left big toe. This creates what is called launch angle and makes it easier to hit a club like a driver up into the air. I really enjoy teaching these little tricks to my senior students, many of whom learned to tee the ball low when they were first starting. I have them just barely stick the tee in the ground and play the ball way up forward in their stance. They use the same swing that was just producing tops and, boom, away it goes, higher and longer. If it is teed up higher, it also gives you more room for error. When the ball is teed too low, we have a much better chance of either topping it or popping it straight up. One is a worm burner, and the other looks more like a chip than a drive.

Look at Figure 5.3. This is just before impact. The big point to be made here is I have not swayed out in front of the ball. This is another one of those things that is important to driving the ball well. I have heard it described as staying behind the ball, but I personally don't like that thought as I have witnessed many golfers who, in trying to stay behind the ball, actually stay back too long and don't follow through correctly. If you stay steady in your swing, you will automatically stay behind the ball. A good drill is again to hit some 5 woods with your feet close together. Separate your feet about 5" at the heels and flare your left foot out. Hit some 5 woods for crispness, not distance. If you sway, chances are you will lose your balance and not experience crisp contact.

Figure 5.3. At impact, I have not swayed ahead of the ball.

Do you have little scratch marks on the top of your wood that you use for tee shots? If you do, then chances are you're doing what is called coming over the top of the swing plane. Most golfers have heard of this but really don't know what it means. I'll explain, so next time you hear it you'll know.

In Figure 5.4, the stick I have stuck in the ground represents the swing plane, that being the path the club takes as it swings back and forth. The part where my body stands is considered below the swing plane, above the stick is the top. When we "come over the top," our swing going back is fine, but on the down swing our shoulders turn first, producing a very steep, outside to inside move that comes "over the top" of

Figure 5.4. The stick represents the swing plane.

Figure 5.5. "Coming over the top" of the swing plane.

the swing plane (Figure 5.5). When we come into the ball this steeply, we hit a glancing blow that pops up, scratching the top of our club head. Often we will hit the ground and even take a divot with our driver which we certainly don't want. Most depressing of all is the fact that we just hit our tee shot 42 yards. One of our friends will always chime in, "I said this hole was a driver, wedge, but I didn't know

Figure 5.6. The hips initiate the down swing.

you were going to hit the wedge first."

So how do we prevent coming over the top, wrecking our beautiful clubs, hitting wedge shots with our driver, and generally depressing ourselves? Here are three drills I like.

First, do some slow motion swings. If your shoulders start the down swing by turning first, then you are coming over the top. Correct this in slow motion. Go to the top of your back swing, then start your down swing with your hips (Figure 5.6). Simple enough. Only in slow motion can you feel this, so only in slow motion should it be corrected. Drill number two is the underhand ball toss. Take a ball in your right hand and set up in your golf stance. Now toss the ball down the target line underhand (Figure 5.7). This is how your shoulders should work in the golf swing. In an over the top move, it's more like you are throwing overhand, which we are trying to avoid. The third drill is the one-hand hit. Take an eight or seven iron in your right hand. Practice with some whiffle balls or crumpled up paper and hit one handed, you will see that your shoulders will start to work correctly soon after you start these drills. Remember to take it easy when you do these or any other drills. Nothing can be learned with a fast, hard swing in practice or in the real game.

Did you know that your shoulders are the sight on your gun? In Figure 5.8 you will notice that my shoulders are aligned straight down the target line. It's amazing how something so simple makes so much difference, especially when you are driving the ball.

I'll never forget going to see one of my fellow professionals early in my career when I thought I had a major problem and I just couldn't figure it out. My

Figure 5.7. The underhand ball toss drill will teach you how your shoulders should work during the swing.

Figure 5.8. Relaxing your right arm at your side is another way to ensure a proper take away. Notice the shoulder alignment, parallel to the target line.

shots were either going high right or low left. I checked my grip, aim, stance, posture, everything I could think of. My wise, experienced teacher asked me to set up to the ball. As I did, I explained the three thousand things I thought it could be and he listened intently. Then he simply held a club across my shoulders, telling me that my gun was aimed at a different target than my eyes were looking at. If I had a gun pointed at a target and I was looking at a different target, the gun would shoot the target it was pointed at, not the one I was looking at. I not only learned a lesson on alignment, but also a lesson in simplicity of teaching. Needless to say, that was the problem and I hit it better instantly.

So back to Figure 5.8. Notice that my shoulders do point down the target line. As the clubs get longer, the ball position moves more forward in our stance. This naturally opens our shoulders to a bad position, open to the target line, which is where we can get in a lot of trouble if we don't adjust for it. To counteract this opening of the shoulders, we must do two things. First, simply crunch your shoulders back to square by putting a club across your shoulders and moving them so the club points straight down the target line. Second, relax your right arm. If we look back at Figure 5.8, we will see that my right elbow is closer to my body than my left arm. From this positon behind me, you can still see some of my left arm. That clearly shows that my right arm is closer to my body. It is relaxed at my side, which puts me in a position to take the club away smoothly and on plane. Most important, it allows me to return to this position at impact. If my right arm is farther away from my body, my shoulders have a tendency to open, and I'm setting up for trouble, especially on the down swing.

In summing up driving, much of what will happen is dictated by our set up. In Figure 5.9F, you can see a good driver set up. Ball position is forward, teed high, right arm is relaxed, shoulders are square, left foot flared, and that set up tilts my shoulders slightly, which it should. From here, we simply swing smoothly toe up to toe up, don't force it, keep your eyes on it, and go to a balanced follow through. Do your drills, practice, and use these tips to learn how to hit it long and straight off the tee. That's a great way to

Figure 5.9.F. Driver set up.

start any hole. Now we will take a look at long irons and fairway woods.

FAIRWAY WOODS AND LONG IRONS

This group of clubs consists of any fairway woods, and long irons down to a five iron. Let's break this group down and explain what each club does and what you can expect to accomplish with each club. The 1 iron is really a club for a low handicap, fast swinging golfer. It requires tremendous precision to hit a long way. I see golfers with these in their bags and they don't hit them any farther than their 5 iron. If that's the case, you are wasting a spot in your bag that a better club could occupy. Now a 2 iron may not be a bad club for you to try. It has more loft than a 1 iron and is great for three shots. The first is the low punch out of the forest when you need to advance the ball a long way and keep it low. The second is for tight tee shots on narrow holes. The third is when you are in a round and your woods are just not working off the tee. That is a good club to practice tee shots with so you have a bail out club that will get you around the course if you are spraying your woods around and getting in trouble. The 3 iron and 4 iron are the same club with slightly more loft. They are easier to hit than a 2 iron and can be used in the same situation.

Pick the one that you feel most comfortable with as your trouble-tee shot-bail out club and put it in your bag. The 5 iron is usually the first club that most senior golfers can reasonably and consistently hit off the ground. I realize how general that sounds, but think about it for a moment. How many good 4 irons or 3 irons have you hit lately? Now think of how many good 5 irons you have hit and it's probably more.

So if we don't have long irons to try to hit off the fairway, what are we supposed to hit when we need to advance the ball way down there? Our fairway woods, of course. We should, depending on our level of play, have a 5, 7 and-or 9 wood in our bag. These woods take the place of long irons and should be a senior golfers' best friend on the fairway. You will notice I did not say anything about a 3 wood for off the ground. The reason is simple. It's a great club for off the tee, but even the best golfers have difficulty with their 3 wood off the turf. It has got too low a loft, it is longer, and requires perfect precision much like a 1 or 2 iron off the ground. You are much more likely to advance the ball solidly with a 5, 7, or 9 wood than a 3 wood. Hitting a 3 wood off the ground is not recommended for all but the best golfers. Back to the 5,7,9 woods. These will take the place in the senior bag of all the long irons above 5.

They are easier to hit, get the ball up higher, land it softer and are generally a lot more fun to use than the long irons off the fairway.

When hitting the long irons and fairway woods, we again need to make a few small adjustments in our set up. For a 5,7,or 9 wood, play the ball about 2" inside your left heel, with your hands slightly in front of the ball (Figure 5.9E). This will create a downward sweeping swing which will pick the ball clean and promote a slight right to left shot. When I'm teaching golfers to hit fairway woods, I remind them how level they must stay to hit it solidly. Look at it this way, you have measured yourself to the ball, are in a good posture with your arms extended, and are balanced. If you stay level throughout the back swing, your body has no choice but to come back to the same spot and pick the ball solidly off the ground. To practice staying level, I like to have my

Figure 5.9.E. 5 wood set up.

students hit fairway woods off either the mat at the driving range, or a tight lie in your yard or wherever you practice. If your level is changing on your back swing, you will top many shots, however, when you can make crisp contact off a tight lie, a real fairway lie is going to seem easy. We will discuss this more in the practice section of this book, but I am a firm believer that you should make your practice progressively harder to prepare you for anything you may encounter on the course. If you are practicing your fairway woods and still topping them, here are two drills to help you.

Get in front of a mirror or sliding glass door and mark where the bridge of your nose is when you are set up. To mark it you can use a crayon or lipstick. Make sure you clear your space so you don't hit anything. Now with or without a club do some gentle back swings, checking to see if your head stays level or not. You will be able to tell immediately, and make the appropriate corrections. If your head is either moving back more than an inch off the ball, or your level up and down is changing, you are in trouble. If that does occur, practice until you can stay level in the mirror before you go to hit more balls. This will help you develop a feel for staying level without the pressure of a ball in the way.

The second drill has two purposes. It will surely teach you how to hit your fairway woods, but it will also show you how versatile they are. Start by chipping, yes chipping, some shots with the highest lofted wood you have. Next hit some 40-yard shots. When you have that mastered, hit some 50 yards, 60 yards, and so on until you reach your maximum distance. This will develop tremendous feel for these clubs. It is important that we become especially good with our fairway woods. As seniors, these are often going to get us either on the green or near it, where our brilliant short game will take over and astound the competition.

There is a great little trick shot you need to know with the fairway woods that I would like to share with you. If you need to hit a low hook (out of the woods, around a tree, into the wind) here is how you do it. Set up with your stance and body aligned to the right of the target. Close the blade slightly, and also when you get your grip see more of the back of your left hand. When you swing, let feel take over, release your hands, and watch it fly right to left and low. What a great little shot. Not that I need to tell you this, but you will want to practice this shot before you try it on the course. Nothing is worse than a trick shot that's not so tricky.

To sum up our fairway woods and long irons, we need to remember a few basics. Never carry a club that you can't hit comfortably, practice a long iron off the tee, practice fairway woods off the ground, stay level and especially get good with those fairway woods. They are the clubs that will put you in position to score.

MIDDLE IRONS AND BALL POSITION

Our next group is our middle irons, the 5,6,and 7 irons. This is the last group before we get down to some serious short game business. These clubs are pretty user friendly and don't give many golfers trouble. It's still important to go over some basics, especially the distance we hit these clubs. Since the 5,6,and 7 are going to be used to hit greens, we need to know how far we hit these with a full swing. Go to a range or an open field with some shag balls. Take the 7 iron and after warming up, hit 10 to 20 shots. Pace off how far to the center of the circle you hit your shots, using one full step as a measured yard. Repeat this process with each club until you have an average distance for each club. This is going to come in handy later when we talk about course management.

Ball position on these clubs, as well as the other clubs, is quite important. If you look at Figure 5.9A-F series of photographs, you will see ball position clearly differs with each of your clubs, if only slightly. No ball position is back of center in our stance, except for trick shots in our short game. On our full swings, sand wedge and pitching wedge start with the ball in the center of our stance, between our heels. From there, as each club gets longer, the ball position moves slightly forward in our stance, with the longest club, our driver, being played off of our left big toe or instep. Think about the different swings and it makes sense why these ball positions are important. When I have a wedge in my hands with the ball positioned in the middle of my stance, my hands are slightly ahead of the ball (Figure 5.9A). This promotes a downward hit which not only gets the ball in the air, but imparts a significant amount of spin on the ball. That is exactly what we want a wedge to do, go high and stop fast. Now suppose I played that same wedge forward in my stance off my left big toe, the position my driver should be. My hands would be behind the ball, promoting an upward swing. The only problem is if I did this with a wedge, I would either skull it, or hit it so high it would hit me in the nose on the way by.

On the other end of the spectrum, if I play my driver off the middle of my stance I have de-lofted the club to a point of negative loft. Any worms or small animals in the area had better run for cover, because it is guaranteed that this set up will produce a screaming grounder. My hands are ahead of the ball and I am promoting a downward swing. That is not conducive to a high-flying drive.

If your ball positions are correct, each club will complement your set up for success. Short irons in the middle will promote level shoulders and a descending shot (Figures 5.9.A and B). A middle iron slightly forward of center promotes a downward but more sweeping swing (Figure 5.9C). Longer irons and fairway woods played off or inside the left heel will give you a sweeping swing that is perfect to pick those clubs off a fairway (Figures 5.9.D and E). And of course, our driver played off our left big toe and teed high will tilt the shoulders correctly and create launch angle (Figure 5.9F). Check and practice these ball positions. If you are having trouble,

Figure 5.9.A. Pitching wedge set up.

Figure 5.9.B. 8 iron set up.

Figure 5.9.C. 6 iron set up.

Figure 5.9.D. 3 iron set up.

use two yardsticks on the range by making a T on the ground that will clearly show you where your ball position is in relation to your stance.

Here is a great way to remember your ball positions out on the course. We know that the shortest clubs, sand wedge and pitching wedge, should be played in the center of your stance. From there, the longer the club, the more to the left heel it moves. Long and left both start with the letter L. Long club, left heel with the ball position. If you struggle with your ball position, that will help.

That sums up the different clubs. You can use this chapter for reference when you are going to practice or to correct a specific group you are having trouble with. Now it's on to the short game where we can take more strokes off our game.

Short Game Sharpness, A Must For Us to Score

I sn't it amazing when you watch professionals play that it doesn't really matter whether they hit the green or not, somehow they can still pull off a par or at worst a bogey. That is the fine art of the short game at work. Because professionals have sound short games, they can swing tension free and with confidence on the approach shots to the green. They are not fearful of the consequences should they miss the green. No big deal, they'll just pitch it close, make the putt, and go on to the next opportunity. Wouldn't it be great if you had that much confidence in your short game? After all, about 60% of the strokes on the score card are shots from 100 yards in. On an average, professionals will hit about 12 or 13 greens in regulation per round. Depending on your game, senior amateurs may hit three or four per round. I'm sure you will agree that puts a premium on having a good short game.

In this chapter I will explain how you can learn to have a professional short game. As seniors, this is not an option. You must have a brilliant short game if you are to stay competitive and have fun. Sure, you may not be able to hit it 300 yards off the tee, but you can earn the respect of everyone you play with if you dazzle them with a precision short game. Not to mention it really shakes up the competition when you keep getting up and down.

When I first started breaking 100, the desire to get better burned inside me. I didn't strike the ball very consistently, but I figured that would come with time and practice. I realized that at the time, I took an awful lot of extra strokes around the green. When I played with better players, they seemed to be much better around the greens. At that point, I decided that having a good short game couldn't hurt, so I started studying how to chip, pitch, putt and get out of a bunker. I took some lessons and practiced. I could have never imagined the change that was about to take place in my game. I was in the mid 80s within three months. My confidence soared as my motto became, "get me anywhere near the green and I'm up and down." To this day my short game is very good and easy to maintain with a minimum of practice. What a great relief to know that even if you are not striking the ball particularly well on a given day, you still can score and more importantly, you can still enjoy yourself.

To finish making my point on the importance of a good short game, I'll share a wonderful story that taught this professional a lesson for life. One of the requirements in earning PGA membership is to pass what is called a Player Ability Test or P.A.T. It is a 36-hole, pressure-filled tournament that is difficult because you know the target score you must shoot, unlike a regular tournament where you just play against the field. So here we are, a group of young bucks, getting ready to tee off and they are calling our names. Three of us are on the tee, but we can't find the last professional in our group. Finally, onto the tee walks this elegant gentleman in his mid 60s and announces he is the pro we have been waiting for. You can guess the rest of this story.

We all crushed our drives a mile except for this nice, seemingly out of place man. I kind of smiled as we waited patiently while he hit first. Funny thing, I thought, he doesn't hit it far, but it sure goes straight. Needless to say, we young guys witnessed the greatest display of short game precision you could ever imagine. This man made it look easy, chip after chip, putt after putt, he got down in two from everywhere. I remember him saying to me that he wished he could hit the ball as far as I, but I think it was just to make me feel good. After 35 holes he was the only one who had a chance of passing the P.A.T., the rest of us missing by a few strokes. The last hole was a par 5 and he needed par. Once again, he was in front of the green in three and after a 30-yard pitch to two feet, he had passed his P.A.T. All us big hitters missed the cut and had to wait until next time. He sure was fun to watch and I learned a great deal.

The three most important lessons were 1) Never judge a book by its cover (although I thought I already knew that!) 2) Distance is overrated, it's accuracy that counts, and 3) Anyone can shoot low scores if they have a good short game. It does not take massive strength, incredible timing, or extraordinary hand eye coordination. It takes knowledge and practice. In this chapter, I will supply the knowledge, and you can take care of the practice. Together we can lower your score now.

CHIPPING AND PITCHING; LEFT, LEFT, LEFT

Chipping will be our first task. If we can get a basic chip shot under our belt, we can expand into all kinds of shots, including some trick shots. A chip shot is a small shot from normally level ground around the green, usually within ten yards, that gets the ball onto the green and rolling as soon as possible. A pitch is a higher lofted shot from usually a little farther away that flies the ball higher over elevation and obstacles to the hole. On a pitch shot, we use our wrists, on a chip our wrists stay firm throughout the shot. Although it's not etched in stone, we normally pitch from the rough and chip from a tight or closely mown lie. Since we are going to develop a significant feel for all of these shots, we don't need to get caught up in the definitions too much. I'm always amused when I hear someone debating whether they should chip or pitch. How about just getting the ball in the hole!

In chipping, we will need to get good with two clubs, an 8 iron and a pitching wedge. If your set consists of 3,5,7, and 9 irons, than use the 9 iron in place of the pitching wedge, and the 7 iron in place of the 8. This gives us two options in chipping. We can hit a high lofted chip with a pitching wedge, or a low running chip with the eight iron. Why only two clubs? I would rather see you get very good with two clubs, than be confused with too many options. We know it takes some serious practice to get a solid chip shot down. We also know that there are an infinite amount of possibilities for short game shots when we use all of our clubs. The problem that I have seen all too often is a golfer with too many options, not knowing which one to choose, and then not having enough experience to execute the option he chose. I could document all the different combinations with all the different clubs, but I don't need to look any farther than my own students to see the futility of such an exercise. Most will practice and even perfect two chip shots, but if I were to hand them a chart with the amount of back swing needed to chip each club a different distance, they would think I was crazy. How much time do you practice the short game anyway? If we keep it simple from the beginning, our options should be limited but effective. So why don't we get good with only one club? We need two clubs to handle the different lies we will be faced with. After we get down the basics, we'll use some other clubs for specialty shots, and through time and experience we will gain the feel to know exactly what club we need to get the job done.

Many golfers have trouble chipping because they try to magically lift the ball into the air, creating an upward swing that skulls the ball across the green into more trouble. Another common mistake is to take too long a back swing and then decelerate coming down, which can also cause a skull. Shifting our weight back and forth during a chip shot can result in a topped chip or even worse the dreaded chunk, which is affectionately called "laying the sod" over the ball. So how do we prevent all these less than desirable outcomes? I teach my students: Left, Left, Left, which will make chip shots a breeze on the course. I'll explain.

When I first started teaching years ago, I wanted to develop easy ways for my students to remember the small things in chipping that make the difference, without having to memorize 50 things, so left, left, left was a natural. We need to think:

Left #1- open your stance to the left of the target.

Left #2- angle the butt of the club to your left pocket.

Left #3- list your weight slightly left and keep it there throughout the stroke.

These three things will be the basics for most of the short game shots that we do, so we will go through them one at a time. Have you ever hit what felt like the perfect chip, only to look up and see it going way to the right of the target? It is very likely that your stance was too square to the target, thereby not allowing your body through and blocking the shot to the right. So the first left is to open your stance to the left of the target. This allows us to clear our hips out of the way when we chip, unlike on a full swing where we are not only farther away from the ball, but also swinging at considerably higher velocity. If we don't open our stance to the left of the target, we have the habit of hitting our chips to the right of the target, or doing the old chunk move. Opening our stance to the left of the target allows the club to move down the target line in harmony with our body action. To open your stance, simply flare your left foot out and drop it back off the target line about 4", then move your right foot into a comfortable position.

The second left is to angle the butt of the club to your left pocket. This is a big one, folks. If you look at Figure 6.1 you will see my stance open and the butt of the club angled toward my left pocket. I can remember when I was learning how hard it was to get my chips into the air. Now I realize that it's no wonder that they would not get up. I was unknowingly breaking the most important basic rule of the short game, for the ball to go up, we must hit down. By angling the butt of the club toward my left pocket, I will

Figure 6.1. An open stance should feel comfortable, and is an important ingredient to the short game shots. The butt of the club is angled left.

come into the ball with a descending blow, hitting down. This will cause the ball to pop up. A question that normally arises at this time is "how much do I angle the club? We don't want to point it way left of our pocket, but it should definitely be to the left of our belt buckle. The farther left we point it, the lower the trajectory of the shot. I think most important is to get the butt of the club pointed left the same amount consistently. This is our bread and butter chip shot and we want the same results each time with no surprises. As we get better at this shot, we can vary the trajectory by the amount we angle the club to the left. If we angle the butt of the club just to the left of our belt buckle, it will give us a slightly higher trajectory than if it is angled to our left pocket. Whatever trajectory you prefer is fine, just make sure you repeat it until you are very good at this shot. Then you can change the trajectories, but by then you have done it enough to let feel take over.

While you are at this point, take a close look at your grip. When you angle the butt of the club to your left pocket, does your left wrist bow and feel uncomfortable? If it does, your left hand grip is in too weak a position, and needs to be corrected by bringing your left hand over more clockwise so you can see more knuckles on the back of your left hand (Figure 6.2). Remember, a weak grip can ruin a chip. Nice little rhyme.

The third left is to list your weight slightly to the left and keep it there throughout the shot. I chose the word list to describe how much you should move your weight to the left because if you overdo it, you can throw your body out of balance. Think of when a ship lists if it has a little too much cargo on one side. When we have our weight listed left, it stays there during the entire stroke. You will never know how many chip shots have failed due to a weight shift that is not supposed to occur. Here is a self-demonstration to prove

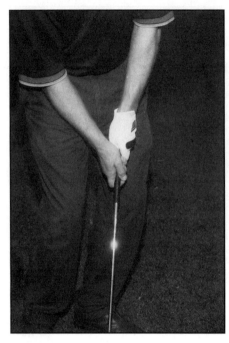

Figure 6.2. A good left hand grip is essential to chip and pitch well.

it to yourself. Do your left, left, left, which is to 1) open your stance to the left of the target. 2) angle the butt of the club towards your left pocket, and 3) list your weight slightly left. Now pick your right heel off the ground (Figure 6.3). Since you are only using your right foot as an outrigger, you can see that it prevents you from shifting your weight. Do some very small chips to get the feel of staying steady. Once you get that feel, practice this drill once in a while until you are staying steady on your chips when you are on the course. When that feeling develops, you will probably never accidentally shift your weight on a chip shot again. This is only a drill, so don't chip like this for any length of time.

Now we need to address what the body is doing during this chip shot. This is a body shot if there ever was one, and you can't chip well or develop feel if your body is stiff. The first thing you will realize when you start chipping is that this shot is a mini golf swing, all the way at the opposite end of the scale from your drive. Even

though it is at the oppo-
site end of the scale, it
still has a great deal in
common with a full
swing, mainly balance
and body motion. We
will discuss balance first.

Just as in the full
swing, the weight must
be on the balls of your
feet. You will see it's even
more important not to
fall onto your heels dur-
ing a chip motion, the
reason being that with a
full swing at least we
have centrifugal force to

Figure 6.3. This drill is designed to teach you to keep your weight on the left side during chip shots.

help hold us into the shot. On a small chip, that centrifugal force is
not nearly as strong, so it's not going to help us if we don't set up
correctly. Notice in Figure 6.4 how I am balanced over the ball.
Back at Figure 6.1, you can see how a good set up looks from the
front, and compare it to your set up in a mirror. In the set up department, there are a few small things that are worth making note
of. In Figure 6.4 notice that my shoulders are level. I see students,
in an effort to get their weight left, shift their lower body to the left
which actually shifts the shoulders and upper body to the right in a
reverse pivot. At this point the right shoulder is considerably lower
than the left shoulder, which causes a dip during the stroke, ending
in a chunk. This will put your body in an unbalanced position and
prevent you from making a downward stroke. If you have ever topped

Figure 6.4. Set up in a balanced posture to chip and pitch.

your way back and forth across the green a few times, this bad balance at set up may be the culprit. Notice I'm also much closer to the ball. Remember that we want to be one hand width from our left leg to the butt of the club on our full swings? That does not hold true for our short game shots. We need to be closer, otherwise our body and arms become disconnected, leaving us with an arms-only swing that tops the ball all over the place. Remember, small shot, small set up.

Here's a great tip for you that has helped many of my students. The size of your set up should match the size of the shot you are trying to accomplish. In these pictures I am doing a small chip shot. My feet are close together, I have gripped down on the club a tiny bit, and the club is much closer to my body than the normal hand width from my left leg. All of these subtle adjustments tell my body that I am hitting a small shot, not taking a full swing. It is especially important to pay attention to the width of your feet. Even if you have a great chipping set up, your feet being too wide apart will send your body confusing signals that you are trying to hit a big shot. Also, the potential for a swing wrecking sway is much more likely if your feet are too far apart. Again remember, small shot small set up. That is another nice, simple thought to remind yourself on the golf course.

Another good piece of set up advice is to level your shoulders to the slope of the hillside if you are facing an uphill or downhill shot. This will effectivily turn all of these shots into level ones, and give you a much better chance of hitting them cleanly. An uphill shot will add loft to your club because of the angle you are launching the ball at, so take one less lofted club. Conversly, if you are chipping or pitching downhill, use a higher lofted club as the downhill lie will take loft off your club. Experience will teach you how the ball will react off these different lies. Remember to level your shoulders to the same angle as the hill side and you will never go wrong on these side slope shots.

We have a nice set up, we have done left, left, left, and we're ready to go. What do we do with our body to get the ball up in the air and on its way? We turn our body and keep our wrists firm. To feel the correct turn, do this nail drill. Hold an eight iron down near the club head (Figure 6.5), with the shaft hovering on the left side of your body. Get into a chipping stance standing up, and do some small chip swings, short back and through, without letting the shaft "nail" the side of your ribs. If the shaft is hitting your ribs, your wrists are breaking down at impact, so try to firm them up as you move your body through the shot. Do this drill and when you start to get the feel of the body motion, let the club resume its full length and try some real balls. You don't really need a target at first, just seeing them go up in the air will be fun. Depending upon your finesse and the temperament of your spouse or room mate, you can practice this inside with those little plastic or foam practice balls. If you break anything, deny you ever read this. Watch out for your pets as they will seize every opportunity to attack the balls.

Now that it's time to hit some chips onto a real green with our new set up, how do we figure out which club to use? Remember

Figure 6.5. Keep your wrists firm and don't nail your ribs.

that we want to get good with an eight iron and pitching wedge to start with. We need to think of the trajectory that we will need for the chip at hand. Is there something in the way that we need to go over, like some rough? Do we need a higher chip that stops, or a long running one? Is the pin close to us or at the other end of the green?

By process of elimination, we can arrive at the correct club to use every time we chip. We will always use our putter when we can. We will use our 8 iron if we can't use our putter, and we'll use our pitching wedge if we can't use our 8 iron. It's putter first, 8 iron second, pitching wedge third. The reasoning is this. From a perfect lie on the fringe, you will probably be able to get a putt closer than a chip. If you must chip, you take a smaller swing with an 8 iron than a pitching wedge, so there is less chance for anything to go wrong. The pitching wedge is the last choice, because it is the hardest to use out of the three and has the greatest potential for a miss hit. I feel it's good to know all this, as I see many golfers use a pitching wedge and hit a bad chip in a situation that would have been perfect for an 8 iron or even a putter. If we make a mistake and blade a club, I would much rather it were an 8 iron, instead of a wedge. If you miss an 8 iron, you didn't take enough swing to get yourself in much trouble, in fact, sometimes it's a pretty good result. A bladed wedge will be much more likely to find trouble simply because we had to hit it harder in the first place. Remember, the object is to get that ball into the hole in the simplest fashion we can find. They don't give out style points.

For chipping around the green, there are two ratios that we need to know. With an 8 iron, we want to land the ball ⅓ of the way to the hole and it will roll the other ⅔ of the way. With a pitching wedge, we will land the ball ½ the way to the hole and it will roll the other ½. This will also help us to figure out what club to use. This way, when we figure out what club and shot we want to use, we will simply try to hit the spot where we want the ball to land, allowing it to roll the rest of the way. These ratios are for level ground. If your shot is uphill or downhill, figure out what you need to add or subtract and hit for that spot. A common mistake is to look at the pin when you are getting ready to chip. This tells your body that you want to land it at the pin, then, even though we hit a solid chip, it's on its way to more trouble. Focus on the landing spot, not the hole. Let's figure out a few scenarios together.

In Figure 6.6, I'm on the fringe cut with a good lie. Regardless of the pin position, if I go down my club list, I don't make it too far before I find the correct club. First, can I use my putter? The answer is yes, so case closed, I will putt. Suppose I am about four yards off the green, with a good lie. The pin is about 10 yards in from the edge of the green. Question number one, can I putt? The answer is no. Even though I have a good lie, I still must get over some rough to get on the green, so the putter is out. Can I use an 8 iron? Well, the total length of the shot is 14 yards. One-third of the way is just under five yards, but I am off the green about four yards. That

Figure 6.6. Putt from the fringe whenever you can.

means that I would have to land it on the green less than two feet from the rough for it to roll correctly to the hole. That's a little too close for comfort, so the 8 iron is out. That leaves the pitching wedge and that is the correct choice. With a little experience, you can figure out each shot mathematically. I will find the spot that is halfway to the hole and try to land it there.

Let's try another scenario. I am about five yards off the green, but the pin is about 15 yards from the side of the green where I'm at. Can I putt? No, I'm in the rough. Can I use my 8 iron? The shot is a total of twenty yards, so ⅓ of the way is about seven yards. I am five yards off the green, so I would have to drop it on the green two yards or six feet in from the fringe to land it ⅓ of the way. That we can do, so I need search no farther, 8 iron is the club for the job. Now it's time to take a few practice swings, do left, left, left, and chip it on the spot I have chosen, then watch it roll to the hole. When the ball stops, I will assess the shot and tuck the results into my memory bank. I try to stay emotionally detached from my shots unless something magical happens, just observe and enjoy. This too we will talk about in more detail, the mental aspects. How do I grade my chips and pitches? If it goes in, it's perfect. If it is within 10% of the total distance of the shot, it was good. Within 20% is acceptable, and outside of that I need more practice. If you have a 30-foot chip and put it inside three feet, you are doing just dandy.

Notice I said take a few practice swings. My reward for getting to my ball quickly is a few practice swings if I am chipping or pitching. On fairway or tee shots, I allow myself one practice swing to feel the weight and length of the club. Chances are I'm using a different club than the shot before and that gives my body a chance to feel the different club in my hands. Since all my full-swing motions are alike, I don't need to rehearse them, just feel the club, so one practice swing will do. On the other hand, when I am doing a short game shot like a chip, I actually need to rehearse it on the spot, because rarely are two chips alike. I will get to my ball quickly, with putter, 8 iron, and pitching wedge in my hand. After making my shot choice, I will allow myself a few practice swings, then let it go. This shot is as important as any shot on the course, so rehearse it well.

Ball position on chips will be about in the middle of your stance, but beware, when you open your stance to the left of the target, it will look farther back in your stance than it actually is in relation to the target line. This has always been confusing. Fight the urge to move it more forward in your stance. A good way to set your ball position is to start your set up with your feet together, ball in the middle, and then open your stance (Figure 6.7). Most golfers who just fish around and set up to the ball, have it too far forward in their stance, making a downward stroke all but impossible. It's easy to blade the ball from here, which can break your heart after you worked so hard to get in position to chip or pitch. So a simple rule is to play the ball in the middle of your stance. The only exception to the middle ball position is if you are on a tight or hard pan

Figure 6.7. Start with the ball position in the middle, then open your stance.

lie. Then we will play the ball back a little farther in our stance to create a more descending shot. Experiment with it until you find the spot that suits you, then practice until you become a deadly chipper. A consistent ball position is another fundamental that will help.

Many students ask me at what distance from the green should you start pitching? That is a tricky question to answer, like someone asking you how far you should drive the ball. It has a lot to do with strength level and power in your upper body. A 40-yard pitch for a professional may be a full swing for someone else. I think we can safely say that as soon as you are forcing chip shots, or if you are hitting to a higher elevation, it is time to pitch. So what's the difference between a pitch and a chip as far as swing motion goes? A pitch uses the same left, left, left as a chip and then adds some things. A chip is a one-lever motion, using only the body but not using the wrists. A pitch is a two-lever motion using both levers, the body and the wrists. We don't want to keep them stiff, we want to relax the wrists and let them hinge naturally. This allows us to come into the rough at a steeper angle than a chip, so grass doesn't get caught between the ball and club face. Secondly, we will make a longer back swing and follow through. It's a bigger shot, so this is necessary. Now we can use our sand wedge, too. We will adjust the length of our back swing to fit the shot. We will see that just like our chips, we need to keep our hands ahead of the ball at impact. If the club head gets ahead of our hands at impact, only bad things can happen.

The first thing we will need to know is how far we hit a full sand or pitching wedge. Suppose we hit our full sand wedge 60 yards. This is important to know, any shot of a shorter distance will be less than a full shot, and we will make adjustments accordingly. For example, if I hit my full sand wedge 60 yards and I have a 30-yard shot to the green from the rough, it would be ½ a full swing. We will adjust this swing with the length of our back swing, and still follow through at least as far as we went back. In other words, if on a pitch I go back to nine o'clock, I must follow through to at least three o'clock. Simple enough. Here is my favorite way to practice pitch shots. We know that we need to develop feel and consistency. Find a place that has some open area and using towels or head covers pace off 10-, 20-, 30-, and 40-yard spots and put a marker. Then shoot for them, but call your shot, you know, 8 iron to 50 yards, sand wedge to 20 yards and so on. You can start by hitting several to each target to develop feel, but then after a while only allow yourself one try at each, just like on the course. It's amazing how much feel you will develop. I always giggle inside when I'm teaching the short game at my present location. There is a target green at 40 yards, 60 yards, and 80 yards. My classes are always amazed that I can just pick up a wedge and actually hit all three greens. It is truly amazing what you can accomplish when you do the same exact shot a zillion times. By the way, those are my favorite distances to pitch on the golf course too. Feels just like home.

In addition to our 8 iron and pitching wedge, the sand wedge, with its heavy weighted bottom, makes it a perfect club to pitch with. The high loft makes it stop fast when it hits the green too. We can chip with a sand wedge, but this should only be attempted after we get very good with our pitching wedge, so we get the idea of accelerating through the stroke. I am a firm believer in progressive learning. If we can get good with our pitching wedge, we at least have a shot that will work under pressure, then we can work on our sand wedge until we can become proficient with that also. For newer students or golfers who may be just learning the correct way to pitch and chip, the sand wedge should only be used if you have some grass under the ball. If the lie is too barren, it is very difficult to pick it cleanly, and you will be better off using an 8 iron or pitching wedge.

Sand wedges come in a variety of lofts, and have something called bounce, which is the angle of the flange on the bottom of the club. Bounce is designed to allow you to hit the sand in a bunker without digging in. That's great if you're in the bunker, but when you are on a fairway that is cut short this bounce can cause a lot of problems. We will get into sand wedges more in the bunker section, but you should plan on carrying three wedges eventually. These would be a pitching wedge of about 50° loft, a fairway sand wedge of about 55° loft with not too much bounce, and a 60° sand wedge with loads of bounce. These high-lofted sand wedges are also referred to as lob wedges, due to their ability to "lob" a high shot into the green. This will give you a complete arsenal for any type of short game shot you can think of.

Before we get back to pitching, I would like to explain in what situation I use each of my wedges. I use my pitching wedge for:

1. Chips and pitches around the green when I don't have to stop the ball very quickly.
2. Pitches to a short pin from the apron in front of the green.
3. Long bunker shots.
4. Full swings to the club's maximum yardage.
5. Bump and run shots to a pin on the front of the green.

I use my 55° sand wedge for these shots:
1. Higher lofted chips and pitches from the rough around the green.
2. Less than full shots from the fairway.
3. Long bunker shots that need to be higher than my pitching wedge.
4. Full swings to the club's maximum yardage.

I use my 60° sand wedge for:
1. High chips and pitches from around the green when there is grass under the ball and I must stop it quickly.
2. High, soft bunker shots.
3. Full swings to the club's maximum yardage from a good lie.

In addition, I use my 8 iron for:
1. Low running chips around the green.
2. Low running pitches if I have enough green to work with.
3. Bump and run shots from anywhere in front of the green where there are no obstacles to go over.
4. Full swings to the club's maximum yardage.

Let's look at some more pitch-shot situations together to get a better idea where we would use each club. In Figure 6.8 I am faced with a slightly uphill shot to a level green and the pin is in the back. I would probably use a pitching wedge because it will go high enough to get on the green, but will release and roll to the hole without stopping too quickly. You will start to get a feel for the right club through trial and error, not to mention experience at the practice area. Sometimes there is more than one correct answer to each situation.

Figure 6.8. Slightly uphill to a back pin will call for a pitching wedge.

What we want to do is find the easiest way to complete the shot. Here is another one. I'm about 15 yards in front of the green with a back pin and a tight lie. Normally, a pitching wedge would be the perfect choice, however we have a tight lie, which makes the pitching wedge a dangerous choice. This is a perfect place to pitch an 8 iron, letting it bump once and release back to the hole. In Figure 6.9 I'm down below the green, and the pin is up just over the edge on my side of the green. Time to use the 60° wedge to stop this ball as quickly as possible once it clears the hillside. Here is another place where the lie told me a lot. It was a nice lie, with the ball sitting up in the grass. If we are going to try a shot like this, we always want to land the ball at least two or three feet onto the green instead of cutting it too close. We all learn that lesson, when we have a delicate chip or pitch, try to get too cute, and wind up with a more delicate one. After practicing these shots for a while, you will realize the many options available to you for each situation. You will also realize that out of all the options, one will yield the best result more often than the others. It's your job to practice all of these shots so you have all the options at your disposal.

Figure 6.9. A 60° wedge will take it high and stop it fast.

A super drill for tempo when you're practicing your pitch shots is the old towel drill. In Figure 6.10, you'll notice the towel draped from armpit to armpit. This will help me move my body and arms together in a connected state, instead of them working independent of each other. When your body and arms work together, you really feel the power a good body turn accomplishes, smoothly and effortlessly. Don't read too much into this drill, it's supposed to be simple. Pitch balls with the towel under your arms. If it falls out, you are swinging with your arms only. Check your balance and try again until you can do it. Some of you will do it right away, and if you do that's fine. When you finish this drill and take shots without your towel on, you should still sense the towel under your arms. Then you know you are swinging with all of your parts working in

Figure 6.10. The towel drill will keep all of your parts moving together in harmony.

harmony. It's a great drill, so have fun.

FUN TRICK SHOTS TO LEARN

I have given you my thoughts and methods for becoming an enviable short game wizard, but now the real secrets will come out. You can't reach golfing euphoria unless you pull off at least one of these shots under pressure. Any one of these shots will dazzle your friends (and you too). The only thing you have to do is get the basic pitches and chips down, and then remember to try these trick shots. Good luck! We'll start simple.

The "out of the woods punch 4 iron" shot = This is simple enough, except nobody practices it so they don't know how hard to hit it. I see many golfers make the mistake of taking too lofted a club from the woods and then hitting a branch. Play a 4 iron in the middle of your stance with your hands slightly ahead of the ball. Now do a standard pitch with a tiny bit of wrist. It will come zipping safely out onto the fairway so you can get back to playing instead of hunting. Practice these little punch shots at the range until you feel comfortable with them. It is feel for the distance that these shots will travel that you are after. There is nothing worse than a successful punch out from under trees that goes across the fairway into more trouble.

The "this ground is so hard, I might as well putt" shot = My father in law and I were playing golf out in Idaho where he lives. He is a new golfer and had overshot a par 3. Now he was facing a down-hill pitch off of hard pan to a green that slopes away from him. With a puzzled look on his face, he asked "What do you think Jim, pitching wedge?," not knowing that even a pro would cringe at the shot he was facing. I suggested he putt down the hard slope and he did with a wonderful result. I think he's still smiling. Don't ever forget that you can use your putter other places than the green, and hard ground is a perfect example. Get the ball to the hole, that's golf.

The "putt from the fringe with a 6 iron" shot. In Figure 6.11, I'm on the fringe but it is too thick for me to use my putter. What I need is a club that will act like my putter but just give me enough loft to clear the collar. That would be my 6 iron. This is another shot you want to practice. It's also fun to try if you're out on the course and not in a major match, until such a time as you are com-fortable and know the result. Take your 6 iron and set up exactly like you would your putter, grip and all. The stroke is the same except you will get a small amount of loft for the first few feet. Hit it with the same force you would use for a putt of the same distance. A wonderful shot to use when the fringe of the green is wet, too fuzzy, or both.

The "stop the club before you bust the shaft against the tree punch shot" = A reasonable alternative to one of the most danger-ous shots in golf, a shot where a tree is in your follow through path. In this next situation, I am in trouble. My ball has come to rest in a place where the only swing I have is to advance the ball toward the

Figure 6.11. "Putt from the fringe 6 iron."

target, but a tree blocks my follow through. What many golfers have tried is to take some sort of swing and stop the club before it hits the tree. Then they get a big surprise when they can't slow the club sufficiently, and hit the tree. This is a dangerous and ignorant shot to take. You can break your shaft, or worse, inflict some serious injury on yourself or your playing partners. Definitely not worth it. So what do we do? The old punch shot. First, without moving the ball, try to ascertain if there are any tree roots in the area of the ball. If there are roots, putt or take an unplayable lie but don't hit it with any major velocity if you will hit a root. If there are no roots, play the club of appropriate loft back in your stance a little, and simply punch it into the ground on impact with the ball (Figure 6.12). Don't try to get the full distance out of your club. The club is going to stop abruptly, so don't hit it any harder than you are willing to take the jolt.

The "I'll never stop this ball near that tight pin from way down here" bump and run. In Figure 6.13, I'm in a pickle once again. I was being a little too aggressive coming into this pin, over shot it and it rolled down this big hill. Now I have this impossible shot that I have to stop on the green, and would really like to stop somewhere in the same area code as the pin. We will do a classic pitch and run. This works for all kinds of situations, and you can use a few different clubs to accomplish it. What we want to do is use the hillside to slow the forward momentum of our

Figure 6.12. "Stop the club before you bust the shaft against the tree."

Figure 6.13. "I'll never stop this ball near that tight pin from way down there." Oh, yes I will!

shot and have it softly bounce once in the rough and release to the hole. We need to figure out how thick the grass is, how far up the hill we want to land it, and how many times it will bounce before it releases onto the green. For instance, in this situation I will use the sand wedge and bounce my ball at the top of the hill because the grass is thick and any more bounces will cause the ball to stop in the rough.

If it were not as elevated, the grass not as thick, and I had more green to work with, I might use an eight iron. You can practice this shot, but once again it is clear that if your fundamental chips and pitches are sound, it will make even this shot seem easy.

The "drop the club onto the ball in the deep rough" shot. This shot applies more to courses with deep rough around the greens. Every once in a while you get a shot where the ball is down in the rough deeper than deep, you can just barely make out that there is a ball down there. When you come upon this tricky situation, use this shot I learned a long time ago. Do left, left, left with a sand wedge, playing the ball back in your stance even with your right foot. Notice in Figure 6.14, there is a very strong angle to my left pocket. Now simply lift the club straight up using mostly wrist motion, then drop it straight down on the back of the ball. It will pop right up out of the rough and onto the green. Practice this shot and develop some touch so you are confident. Where I see many amateurs make their mistake in this shot is to try some fancy lob shot and have the rough grab their club, resulting in a clunk or whiff. Keep it simple and score.

The "it's so windy I need to keep this ball low" 4 iron punch shot. Re-

Figure 6.14. "Drop the club onto the ball in the deep rough."

member that old saying, "When it's breezy, swing easy?" That is true. We need to think of trajectory when we are playing in the wind. Suppose I am about 80 yards from the green, in the fairway, good lie, with no major obstacles to go over, and a major wind in my face, about 30 mph. Instead of throwing a sand wedge as a sacrifice to the wind and hoping that I can find it, I will control the situation by pitching a 4 iron low into the wind, bouncing once or twice on the apron, and letting it roll onto the green. This can also be used on a day when you are hitting your short irons poorly but can't seem to correct it. At least you will be able to enjoy your round with the 4 iron pitch. Again set up left, left, left, and play the ball in the middle of your stance with your hands slightly ahead of the ball. Use the amount of wrist needed to hit it the distance you need. Another benefit of practicing this shot is you may surprise yourself and actually get a good feel for your long irons.

The "sure I can use the cart path" out of the woods bump shot. I can personally vouch that this shot will leave all those who are watching in awe, including yourself. I've been here before, stuck in the woods across the cart path with no shot. To make matters worse, there are overhanging branches which make taking this shot to the air impossible. Using a standard pitch shot, I'm going to let this ball bounce off the cart path, hit the hill to slow it down, and land on the green, by then rolling slowly. How hard do you hit it? You will have to decide. Which club shall I use? Think of the trajectory you need, then try to make the right decision. More than likely you will use a mid iron, 6 or 5 iron, to get it high enough to get of the trouble, but low enough to miss the overhanging branches. Use feel and imagination, but again, if you are confident with your pitches and chips you can have the imagination to see shots where others cannot. Then you only need to pull them off.

THE CUT SHOT

The last trick shot goes hand in hand with bunker play, so we will learn this shot first on dry land then take it to the sand. It's the "I saw a guy on t.v. do this" cut shot. After we have control of our pitches and have developed good feel, we all need a shot that goes high by opening the blade of a sand wedge. In my humble yet experienced opinion, the problem that most golfers encounter with this shot is not a lack of talent, but rather a good solid method to get into the same position each time they try it. The same holds true for bunker play. Even though the shot is not difficult, getting into a good set-up position seems to be most elusive to the average golfer. After struggling with my own bunker play early in my career, which I will explain later, I came up with this little rhyme that really works for both the cut shot and bunker play. We will apply it to a cut shot from the grass first. It goes;

SQUARE, SQUARE

OPEN, OPEN

HANDS AHEAD

FOLLOW YOUR FEET

To this day I use this every time I do a bunker shot or this cut shot. I feel a good preshot routine is critical to playing a shot well and this little saying gets me into the right position. Let's walk through this process together. SQUARE, SQUARE (Figure 6.15). Our stance is square to the target, and our blade is square to the target line. Notice that my feet are together, I am the correct distance away from the ball, and I am balanced on the balls of my feet. This is the aiming part of the cut shot. If my stance is square to the target at the beginning, then I know after I open my blade and stance, they will counteract each other to the target line that I started on, my aiming point. If I just get up and open the blade and my stance without any precision, I'll get a different result each time, which I don't want. Back to SQUARE, SQUARE. We have established where we want the ball to go. Now for the loft, OPEN, OPEN. From our SQUARE, SQUARE position, we need to open the blade to affect the loft and bounce on the club.

Figure 6.15. SQUARE, SQUARE.

How do we open the blade? By rotating the club ever so slightly in our fingers, not by moving our whole hands. This is so important that I have given you more fun pictures (Figure 6.16) so you can see what I mean. How much do we open the blade? As you gain more experience it will vary, but about 30° open or 1 o'clock is a good place to start. Look at the blade of the club in relationship to the target line now. It's open, but aimed to the right. If I hit the ball now, where would it go? If you said dead right, you're dead right. The only way we can get this blade lined up to the target is to open our stance, so that the leading edge of the club is square to the target (Figure 6.17). O.K., we've gotten this far, only two small things left. Notice that when I opened my stance, it put my hands back behind the ball? To ensure a descending shot, we now must press our hands slightly ahead of the ball (Figure 6.18). Now we are

Figure 6.17. Open your stance so that the blade once again aims to the target.

Figure 6.18. Hands ahead of the ball to ensure a descending shot.

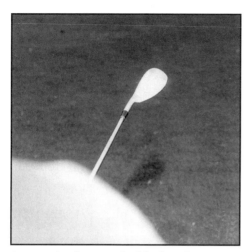

Figure 6.16. Open the blade 30˚ or to one o'clock.

ready to pull the trigger. Swing the club along the line of your feet (Figure 6.19), and hold the rotation in your hands. In other words, don't let the toe of the club roll over past the heel until after impact.

They call this a cut shot because you cut across the ball, and it comes out high and soft. A word of warning; you need a good lie in the grass to successfully pull off this shot. Remember that we professionals only do this shot when there are no other options left. We don't do this every time we pitch, only when we have a good lie and must use it.

Start practicing this shot either fluffed up in some nice grass or on a tee sticking about ½" out of the ground. As you get better, lower the tee and try to dig it out of some tougher lies. It really is a feel shot. When you get it down, you will have a shot in your bag that will hit the ball high and land it softly, not to mention how it goes hand in hand with our bunker shots, which sounds like a swell place to go from here.

TO SUM IT UP

Before we go to the bunker, let's review our chips and pitches. We will be left, left, left, on all these shots. That is stance opened to the left of the target, butt of the club angled to our left pocket, and weight slightly left. Our weight stays left throughout the shot. We turn our body and keep the wrists stiff on chips. We can use our wrists on pitches. We will use the 8 iron, pitching wedge, and sand wedge, depending on the shot and trajectory we need. The distance our feet are spread apart will be dictated by the size of the shot we are doing. We will always putt first, use the 8 iron if we can't putt, and use a wedge (sand or pitching) if we can't use an 8 iron. The towel drill and nail drill will help us learn to use our body properly. We need to get down a basic chip and a basic pitch before we start to get fancy. When we do get the basics down, work on some trick shots so that we always have a trick up our sleeve. Develop feel and use lots of imagination. Practice until you have a magical short game and are confident from anywhere around the green. Then you will see your scores drop, and will be able to play with the big hitters knowing that you have a chance of beating anyone.

Figure 6.19. Follow your foot line when you swing.

7

Getting Good From Bunkers

I hate to say it, but usually something drastic has to happen in our games to make us work harder and learn to do something the right way. A big number on a hole, or even just the embarrassment of totally losing control when you were on a good game can set it off. No one I know likes "to stink the course up." As golfers, we all have those moments of disbelief at our inability to master a particular shot. In my position as a P.G.A. professional and teacher, I can think of no more glaring example of this than bunker play. In playing with students, this is an area that really strikes fear into many of them. It must be the fact that we're not called upon to do this shot very often. You may go a whole round or two without getting in a bunker. Also, if you look at the grand scheme of golf, certainly driving, putting, chipping, pitching, and fairway woods will take priority over some shot that you may only use once in a while. I don't see many golfers practicing bunker shots, but if one doesn't know how to negotiate a particular shot, practicing it usually ends in frustration and loss of interest. Most of us would rather see tee shots flying into space, rather than a little shot and some sand flying ten yards. But it is the psychological fallout of a bad bunker shot on the golf course that concerns me, especially for senior golfers. For instance, you are playing along nicely and having fun. You're not breaking the course record, but this could be a pretty good round. Then you get to a par 4 that you can reach in two, and you hit a great drive. The second shot calls for a 5 wood if you're going to reach, and you go for it. Great shot, but it just catches the top of the bunker and rolls back in. Too bad, another foot and it would have made it, but this is a very common scenario for senior golfers with long second shots. This is also where it's up to you how the rest of the story goes. Since bunker play doesn't require any more strength and agility than it takes to hit a 30-yard pitch, here's how I would like this story to continue. Walking up the fairway with your buddies, you are confident that your upcoming shot will be good. So much so, that you are not even thinking about it, just enjoying the walk. As you approach the bunker, you see that the ball is on a good lie, but there's a high lip to this bunker. You think to yourself "I have to come in steep to get this ball up." After you settle in, whoosh, out pops the ball to eight feet. You are satisfied because you know the worst you're going to do is two putt for bogey, and you think to yourself "now is a good time to make a putt." Then you drain it!

A BUNKER SHOT THAT WORKS

Here is the other scenario. You walk up the fairway cursing yourself for ever trying such an impossible shot. "Why did I go for it, now look what I've done." You already have a bad attitude as you approach the bunker because your bunker play is less than stellar, then you see the lip and really panic. With trepidation you climb into the bunker and yell "heads up." The first one chunks about a foot, but you knew that was going to happen. Now you are really close to the lip, so you give it all you got and it plugs under the lip. Swat number five is a whiff and about that time you say "you guys go ahead and play, I'm picking up." This adventure will follow you the rest of the round. Which golfer are you? Which would you like to be? In my career I have been both. You see, good bunker play not only gets you out of a bunker, but can greatly affect your decisions on shot choice and your confidence level in making those shots. On most of the approach shots we take, bunkers will be lurking nearby. We can't let that scare us. If we are fearful of landing in a bunker, we can't take a confident swing at our approach shot.

In a way, we should be able to look at a bunker as a friend. First of all, it's the only hazard on the golf course that we really stand a chance of getting out of without a penalty. It's the only shot that we really don't want to hit the ball. Sometimes the bunker can actually save us a stroke or two. I can think of many times that the only thing keeping my ball from rolling down a hill into the water was a bunker. As any pro will tell you, if we're shooting at a green with O.B. or water on one side and a bunker on the other side, we want to miss on the bunker side if we hit a bad shot. We need to look at bunkers as just another shot, like a chip or a putt, and not a torture test.

The turning point in my bunker play came in a tournament in Orlando early in my career. On a par 4, I hit my second shot in a green side bunker, nothing special, and faced a routine sand shot to a middle pin. At the time, I considered myself to be an adequate bunker player but I guess I was wrong. I bladed my first shot across the green, but to add insult to injury it came to rest out of bounds. Hitting five, I sure wasn't going to put this next one O.B. and I didn't. The only problem was that I overcompensated and left this one in the bunker. Number six at least got out, and I promptly three putted for a smooth running nine. It's amazing how frustration and embarrassment are such wonderful motivators, isn't it? After ruining my round and beating myself up for a while, I decided that this would not happen again if I had anything to say about it.

Something else was going on around the same time. When asked to give a bunker lesson, I would jump in and explain all that I knew about bunker play. I would hit mostly good demo shots and then, after explaining about the opened blade and foot line, the students would hit some good ones too. Off the student would go armed with encouragement and their newfound knowledge. Then I noticed a pattern begin to develop. When I asked any student who had taken a bunker lesson how they were coming along, they sheepishly replied "not too good." Did you practice, I asked? All of them said they did, but were still not getting it. Now as a person who stakes his reputation on helping golfers get better, this was most distressing news. Why weren't they getting it? Why could I hit great bunker shots in practice and lessons, but not under pressure? After thinking about it, I realized that the only difference between my bunker shots and the regular shots I hit were the frequency with which I used them. Again, it wasn't lack of talent or knowledge. The problem is to be able to confidently reproduce a shot that you don't use often, but can be very damaging if you miss. So if the answer didn't lie in the stroke itself, where was it? Some more pondering made me realize that the reason most of my other shots went well was the frequency that I did them, and my solid preshot routine that gets me into the same position every time I hit. Frequency didn't make sense. If that was the case, why did I hit my 2 iron well when I only used it occasionally? Then it dawned on me! I needed a preshot routine that could be pulled out on demand, that would produce a good bunker shot. The problem was the bunker shot is so complicated that a preshot routine could not possibly cover it all. After some experimentation, I settled on a good one and proved to myself once again that a good teacher had better not stop learning. I have been using it with my students ever since, with wonderful results. I will explain it in depth to you, and the only thing I ask is that you memorize this rhyme (which is the same for a cut shot from a good lie);

SQUARE SQUARE
OPEN OPEN
HANDS AHEAD
FOLLOW YOUR FEET

We will review this before we get into different lies, fairway bunkers, and specialty shots from the sand. We need to define where we are aimed, and square, square does this. In Figure 7.1 my blade and stance are square to the target line. This, by the way, is how our preshot routine will start for all of our shots. This is when we measure ourselves to the ball (remember, one hand width from the butt of the club to our body), and make sure we are balanced on the balls of our feet (feel nice and springy). So far it's SQUARE the blade and SQUARE the stance. OPEN, OPEN is our

Figure 7.1. SQUARE, SQUARE in the sand.

next step. On the bottom of your sand wedge is a flange called bounce. This is what enables your club to bounce off the sand taking the ball with it, instead of digging in and stopping. Try this drill. Holding the club with both hands, keep the blade square, swing it lightly and hit the sand. See how it digs in? That's because when the blade is square, your sand wedge acts like any other club and the bounce doesn't work. Now open the blade a little and do the same swing. Notice how the club bounces off the sand. You have affected the bounce and "turned it on" so to speak. Figure 7.2 clearly shows the bounce affected when the blade is open. We open

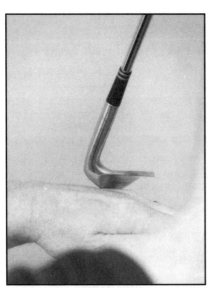

the blade by turning the club in our hands. If the blade is at 12 o'clock when it's square, it should be at 1 o'clock to be open. After we get some experience, we will probably open it with slight variations for the type of shot we want. For now, we want a shot that works every time, so 1 o'clock is fine. Therefore our first OPEN is to open the blade to 1'oclock by turning the club in our fingers, not moving our hands around.

Figure 7.2. The bounce is affected when the blade is open.

If you look where the club is now pointed, if you hit it, the shot will go right. We need to OPEN our stance to the left so that our blade points once again at the target (Figure 7.3). Spread your feet, flare your left foot out, and open your stance counterclockwise until the blade points to the target. (An open stance means that your left foot is dropped back

Figure 7.3. Open your stance so the blade aims at the target again, just like the cut shot in the grass.

off the target line more than your right foot). Wiggle your feet a bit, until they dig into the sand so we can establish a firm stance. We don't want to slip when we swing. Now we put our hands ahead so that we create a descending shot that hits the sand. Here comes the tricky part that makes this shot so different. We have been releasing our wrists (rolling them over at impact) to generate more club head speed. On this shot we don't roll them over. We never let the toe of the club pass the heel during a regular bunker shot. We also FOLLOW YOUR FEET, which is to swing outside to in along your foot line. That completes the bunker preshot routine:

SQUARE the blade

SQUARE your stance

OPEN the blade

OPEN your stance

HANDS AHEAD

FOLLOW YOUR FEET

We need to start somewhere, so we are going to hit some small cut shots off a low tee to feel what this shot feels like. Notice something very important. My follow through on all of these shots is longer than my back swing. One of the quickest ways to blow a bunker shot is to decelerate on the down swing and stop at the ball. The same goes for our little cut shot. After popping a few off a tee (Figure 7.4), find some fluffy grass and hit some from there. As soon as you are comfortable with that shot, it's time to tackle the sand. Find a friendly practice bunker, and draw some dollar bill-size squares in it. I know, the rules state that you can't touch the sand, but we are only practicing. Now go through your preshot routine on each shot (You know, SQUARE, SQUARE, etc.), squish your feet in a little, and splash your dollars out of the bunker, with a smooth swing and a flowing follow through. You can see that to accomplish this, you need to swing with a controlled aggression. We can't baby this shot. We are going through a very thick substance unlike any other on the course, so we have to swing with some zip. This is another point that confuses the average golfer. You must swing as if you are going to hit it

Figure 7.4. Hit some cut shots off a tee first.

80 yards, but it only goes 10. That is because the club never touches the ball, it simply scoops the piece of sand the ball is sitting on.

There are two ways to create enough club head speed to hit effective bunker shots, and it all depends on your strength level. If you have a strong upper body, hands, wrists, and forearms, or have a short swing to begin with, your bunker swing will be shorter and more aggressive. If you do not possess that strong upper body, or have a longer, smoother swing for your regular shots, then by all means use a longer swing in the bunker. A bunker shot is odd enough to understand, without complicating it further by adopting a different style of swing than you already use. Use your style, not someone else's.

Now that you have hit some dollar-size squares out, we can move on to something more solid. I like to crumple up some aluminum foil into golf ball size balls for my students to try if a real ball makes them nervous. Line up some balls in the bunker, and make a line about one inch behind them with the rake handle. Now when you hit, focus your eyes on the line, not on the ball (Figure 7.5). This is a super drill to get used to looking at the sand behind the ball. On a few shots your

Figure 7.5. Look at the line when you practice, not the ball.

focus will drift back to the ball, but you will be reminded by the ball going like a rocket off your club face. Believe it or not, I like to look at the smallest thing 1" behind the ball that my eyes can see; a grain of sand, a stone, a piece of shell, anything to keep my eyes off the ball. From here it's practice until you develop a feel and can get the majority of the real balls that you practice with out of the bunker and onto the green. To get good at a routine bunker shot, it requires a long practice session the first time you really get serious about learning it. I would recommend spending a morning playing shots from a bunker. Take lots of breaks so you remain interested. That should be sufficient time to develop a feel for a basic sand shot. Then if you practice a few shots every time you are hitting balls, you will retain the feel needed to pull it off on the course. Never be afraid to hit bad shots when you practice. We would rather get the bugs out on the range than not be confident on the course. Remember, for you newer bunker players, any bunker shot that winds up on the green is a good shot.

I have good news for you. If you get one bunker shot down, any variations are easy. Also, once you become decent at bunker play, it's easy to maintain with just a little practice. It's the concept that is difficult, not the shot itself. For these reasons, I always look behind the ball the same distance, 1", and vary the length of my shots by three things; the velocity I swing at, how open my blade is, and how steep I come into a shot. As you get better, you will start to experiment with these variables too. Opening the blade adds loft to the sand wedge, but there is a point where you can over do it. For short shots, come in swinging at a steeper angle, for longer shots, swing on a more shallow angle. For long shots, take a little less sand and swing harder, for short shots, swing a little softer and take more sand. An ever important note is to always have more follow through than back swing to insure acceleration. Again, start experimenting with these different variables AFTER you get a standard bunker shot down. Imagine how wonderful it will be to have a bunker shot that you can reasonably count on to get out of the bunker and on to the green most of the time. Good bunker shots instill tremendous amounts of confidence every time you do one. Practice up, learn this shot, and never fear a bunker again. Now we will address some interesting bunker situations that we can use fun trick shots to impress your friends again, just like in chipping and pitching.

First of all, how do we know what the sand is like in a bunker without touching it? We must "listen" to our feet when we walk in the bunker and take our stance. From here you have to make decisions based on feel. Here is an all too familiar scenario. You look in the bunker and see that your ball has not even pierced the surface of the sand. Upon closer inspection, you find the sand in the bunker is wet and hard. First of all, you don't want to open the blade too much or you will create too much bounce and skull this poor ball. To counteract this, you should come in steep to get the ball up and out. It will likely come out lower and faster than a normal dry bunker, so allow for some extra roll. That's one option. Let's use imagination and look at another way to handle this situation. If there is no major lip in between my ball and the hole, you can use a sneaky trick that is often forgotten in the heat of battle. The sand is hard, so why not putt it out, using the face of the bunker as a launch ramp? Visualize the shot, shoot it up the ramp, let it bounce once on the fringe, and roll toward the hole. My students get a huge kick out of this shot, once they try it. The only thing you have to do is remember that you have that option when you're in a hard surfaced bunker, and then do it. It's loads of fun and the results may surprise you.

FRIENDLY FAIRWAY BUNKERS

Fairway bunkers are not as deadly as everyone thinks. The mistake most golfers make is not to get good footing by squishing your feet down into the sand a little. This gives you a good base to hit from. If you have a good base to hit from, you can keep your lower body relatively quiet during the swing. Where many golfers get into trouble is when their lower body moves too much during a fairway bunker shot. When your lower body moves, your feet can sink into the sand more as you swing, lowering your elevation as you come into the ball. A lower elevation may cause you to hit behind the ball, moving it only a fraction of the distance that a clean pick would have. What other adjustments would I need to make? Well, if we squish our feet down into the sand, we need to grip down on the club the same amount that we have dug our feet in. Play the ball in the middle of your stance. Stay level and pick it. That is my swing thought as I hit these shots and try to pick them clean. What club should you use out of a fairway bunker? It all depends on the sand and your lie. Fairway bunkers should be hard sand, so you can hit a fairway wood (5 wood maximum, no 3 woods) or up to about a 5 iron, if you stay level and pick it clean. If the sand is fluffy, you can only pitch out like a regular bunker shot. Try to find a place to practice these shots. They are really loads of fun to play once you get some experience behind you. If you do have a course to practice at during the off hours when it's not too busy, practical experience will help. If you are out practicing, try a few shots from a real fairway bunker. As long as you are not holding anyone up, the experience will help you overcome any fear of fairway bunkers that you may still have. When you learn to pick these shots clean, you will see that you can hit your ball the same distance from a good lie in a fairway bunker as you can from the fairway. It will only take some practice.

PLUGGED IN THE LIP

Here's a situation I wouldn't wish on anyone (Figure 7.6). My approach shot came up short and I have plugged myself into the face of the bunker. To most golfers, a lie like this would bring tears to their eyes, for they know disaster is not far off. However, if you know how to negotiate this shot, it's not real hard. Since we know all of us are going to need this shot sooner or later, if we prepare correctly we will be able to handle it. Not to mention, this is really impressive to your playing partners. Guaranteed when you calmly pull this shot off, your friends will beg you to teach them how you did it. First of all, we need to determine if there is a chance to get this ball out. A good rule of thumb is this; if the angle of the bunker face is more than about ten o'clock, don't try it. In other words, if

Figure 7.6. Plugged in the face of the bunker. What now?

the wall of the bunker is straight up and down (twelve o'clock), or anywhere near that, don't attempt it. If it is ten o'clock or less, we can do this shot. We need to climb up the wall so the ball is even with our right foot instep (back in our stance). Open your stance slightly and keep the blade square. Squish your feet in to get a solid base. Depending on how high up the face of the bunker the ball is, your left foot may even be outside the bunker, and that is fine. Level your shoulders as close as possible with the slope of the sand. Now you're ready to go. Look 1" behind the ball and hammer it. There is no follow through because you whack the club right in to the face of the bunker 1" behind the ball and that's it. The club will stop abruptly, a whole pail full of sand will fly, and somewhere in the middle of all that sand will be your ball gently floating toward a soft landing. Great shot, and it really works!

How about if there is more than a ten o'clock angle on the face of the bunker? Suppose it's straight up and down and your ball is plugged in the wall? Here is one of those times when it's a good idea to know the rules and use them to our benefit. We have several options, most of which will cost us a stroke. What we don't want to do is compound the problem and take a big number out of frustration and anger. Our inner self tells us to start beating at the ball until we get it out, which, in fact, is one of our options. Normally that is the first option that many amateurs choose, with disastrous results. If you are sure that you can safely play out sideways on your first try, go for it. If there is any doubt in your mind, take one of the other options. The way I look at it, we hit a bad shot or picked the wrong club to put us in that position to begin with. So what, we're only human! Losing one shot is a sufficient penalty, not taking a nine on the hole. Here is where we use the rules to get us out of a jam. According to rule 28, we can declare our ball unplayable. Then we have three options:

1) We can play a ball from as nearly as possible from where we played our last shot.

This may be a good option if you are more confident from the fairway, you are in a particularly treacherous bunker, or your last shot was not very long. I don't know that I would use this option if I had hit a long iron or wood past a lot of trouble to reach the bunker. If I had used a shorter club, a 7 iron for instance, I may consider going back and using a 6 iron.

2) Option number two allows us to drop a ball within two club-lengths of the spot where the ball is, but no closer to the hole.

This also may be a good option. You must drop the ball in the bunker, but if it's a pretty friendly bunker and you feel confident, do it! This would not be a very good option if the wall was so high that two club-lengths back still didn't give you a reasonable shot. Again, you have to make the call.

3) Option number three sounds a lot like number two, but it differs slightly. You may drop a ball behind the point where the ball is plugged, keeping the spot where it's plugged between the hole and the spot where the ball is dropped.

What does all that mean? This is a great choice if there is a wall or steep face on the front of the bunker where your ball is plugged, but it's a long bunker. As long as you drop it in the bunker and keep the plug spot in between you and the hole, you can go back far enough to get away from the wall and give yourself a shot. So there are three options you can use instead of chopping at a plugged ball in a bunker wall. Read the rules and become familiar with them.

SPECIALTY SHOTS

Suppose you have a downhill lie in a bunker. It normally occurs when a ball just rolls in to the back of a bunker and doesn't have enough velocity to make it to the bottom. Not a real friendly shot, but we have to get it out. Play the ball back in your stance, put your weight to the left, and once again level your shoulders to the slope of the sand. The tricky part is to hit down and through following the slope. If you try to lift this shot out, you'll launch it like a rocket into the next county. Surely a shot worth practicing.

Ever have a fried egg? Not the breakfast one, a fried egg lie in a bunker. This is a fairly common occurrence when you hit a high shot at a green, it comes up short, and lands in a bunker filled with soft sand. It's called a fried egg because the ball hits the sand with such velocity, it splashes the sand into a halo around the ball and looks just like an egg, with the ball being the yolk. The soft sand that causes the fried egg lie to begin with can only help us get the ball out since it's not too hard. I hear many different theories on how to do this shot, but I like to keep it simple. Do your regular bunker shot and make these small changes. Squish your feet down extra to dig deep, and don't open the blade at all. Put about 75% of your weight on your left side, and play the ball back in your stance, even with your right foot. Come in steep and dig it out. A major point is to allow for more roll since it will come out lower and hotter. Could it hurt to step on a few balls in the bunker during practice? I should say not. After you get familiar with this shot, you will be able to identify when and how much you can open the blade for this shot. You will also develop some feel.

TO SUM IT UP

Let's review our bunker shots. We know that for a regular bunker shot our pre shot routine will be SQUARE, SQUARE, OPEN, OPEN, HANDS AHEAD, FOLLOW YOUR FEET. Looking 1" behind the ball, we will hit the sand with some solid velocity, not let the club roll over, and follow through. For fairway bunkers if the sand is hard and we have a good lie we want to pick it cleanly by focusing in on staying level throughout the swing. If the sand is soft or we have a bad lie in a fairway bunker, the only thing we can do is a regular bunker shot. Sometimes we will be able to putt out of a bunker if the sand is hard and there is no huge wall to stop our ball. For a ball buried in the face, we need to determine if there is less than a ten o'clock angle and if there is we can go for it. We keep the blade square and whack it into the wall just below the ball. Any time we do a sand shot from a slope in the bunker, we must level our shoulders to the same angle of the slope. If there is more than a ten o'clock angle, chances are we will not get it out. That is when we declare the ball unplayable and take whichever of the three options suits our needs. A fried egg lie calls for us to dig it out and allow for it to run when it hits the green.

As seniors, many of the approach shots we take have the potential of landing in a bunker, because we are often hitting long clubs into the green. If we are to stay competitive, we need to have a sharp short game. This includes bunker play. If we can get that basic bunker shot down, we will realize that we can in fact do it, we'll gain confidence, and probably look forward to practicing, knowing that we actually stand a chance of getting out. The level of confidence in our approach shots to the green is directly proportional to the quality of our short game. Good luck and don't let those bunkers intimidate you any more.

C H A P T E R **8**

The Fine Art of Putting

How important is putting? We can put it this way. If you average more than two putts per hole, you're not doing yourself or your score any favors. That would be 36 putts per 18 hole round. For most amateurs, that would cause a significant drop in their scores. This is another part of the game that you can be as good at as any professional in the world. Putting only takes skill and practice and anyone can get better at it. If you happen to be one of the lucky ones who putts well, you still want to check out what's in this section. I am sure you will find something that will take a few more strokes off your score.

You've heard me say this before, but it is worth repeating. Senior golfers must be good putters if they are to be competitive with the big hitters. Good putting can keep you in the game, and can even intimidate the long hitters a little. They know that if you are a great putter, you can take advantage of your good putting more often than they can take advantage of their length. Chances are they will hit into trouble before you 3 or 4 putt. We know that our short game has to be sharp, but we need to be able to back up a great chip, pitch, or bunker shot with a one putt, or two putt at worst. This again will keep us in the game. I feel we can always search for a few extra yards off the tee, but we should look for extra yards only after we become great putters. Chances are at this point in our careers, it's a heck of a lot easier for us to become brilliant putters rather than long drive champions, although both would be nice ....

WHAT IS GOOD PUTTING?

When I am doing putting clinics, I am always surprised by the number of putts golfers take on the course. I'll ask a volunteer to go over their last nine hole round with me and the rest of the class. We will go hole by hole and count their putts. It's very common for me to ask "How many did you take on the first hole?" and hear them answer "Three. O.K., how about the second? Three. The third hole? Four." This will go on until we have counted all nine holes and come up with the number of putts she had during the last nine holes she played. I will ask her score, which we will say is 57, for example, with 25 putts. Now if she took off eight putts per nine holes, which is easily obtainable, it would leave her with an average of 34 putts per 18 holes, she could lower that 57 to a 49. To put it into a stronger perspective, the first golfer would shoot 114 with 50 putts. The new, improved putter would shoot 98 with 34 putts. I don't know about you, but 98 for 18 holes or 49 for nine holes looks a lot more appealing than 114 or 57. Now suppose you say, "Jim, I shoot in the high eighties and low nineties and feel like I putt pretty well." That's fine, except the combination between tweaking up your short game and then putting well has to lower your score. What do you think would happen if you and I went out to play and we did an experiment? You hit all your regular tee shoes and approach shots. I will hit all your shots from inside 100 yards, all pitches, chips, bunker shots and putts. What do you think you would score? I would imagine it would be a bit better than your normal score. One of the major differences would be putting. Most professionals average in the high twenties or low thirties in putts per round. Think back to your last round. Go hole by hole and try to remember how many putts you had. If it was more than 17 per nine, we have room to improve with a minimum of effort.

I like to tell my students this story, as it tells of the value of a good short game. My dad and I played Pasadena Yacht and Country Club, a beautiful track with a lot of history near my school in Tampa Bay. It was a few years back and very, very windy, gusts 40 mph, but warm. When you hit the ball a long way, the wind can really throw it around. That day I only hit three greens in regulation, but shot 75 from the back tees. Certainly not my lowest round, but a wonderful testament as to how a good short game will keep you interested and having fun, which we did. I realized early on in that round that the wind was going to make hitting the greens difficult. My plan was to get the ball close to the green, keep it out of trouble, then let my short game take over. My plan worked beautifully. It did make me think of something along the way that directly applies to my senior students. I could only reach a few greens that day due to my disadvantage (the wind), yet still managed a great score, thanks to my short game. The wind is no different a disadvantage than not being able to reach some of the greens due to lack of distance of our shots. That's when I realized just how important the short game would be to senior golfers, if they were to still shoot low scores. A major part of that short game is putting. Often underestimated, putting accounts for more than 40% of the strokes that you will write on your scorecard. No matter how good we think we putt, we can always get better.

GRIPPING THE PUTTER

Notice in the equipment section we did not discuss putters. I feel that to be fitted properly for a putter, you must know how to grip the putter correctly. It is a different grip than you use for your regular swing. We need to learn how to grip the putter correctly before we can see if our putter fits us. We will learn the putting set up and stroke, then we'll find that perfect putter for us.

There are several different putting grips and variations that we can use. These are all different than the way we grip the rest of our clubs and for a good reason. If we grip our putter like the rest of our sticks, we are telling our body that we want to swing the putter, when in fact we want to stroke the putt. Additionally, if we use a standard grip, we tell our body we want to use our wrists, which we will see can wreck our ability to judge distance. Finally, a standard grip will prevent us from getting our eyes over the ball, resulting in a lot of misdirected putts.

I like my students to learn either the reverse overlap grip or the cross handed grip. Both are very effective and help take the wrists out of the stroke. The reverse overlap is my first choice. I think it's an easier grip for newer golfers to master. If you have a bad putting grip now, this is a good grip to go to. The cross hand grip is good for someone who wants to breathe new life into their putting stroke; maybe a player who has been playing a while, and would like a change. Feel free to try them both. The beauty of putting is that it's not an exact science. As long as the basic criteria are met, the rest is style, feel, and practice.

The reverse overlap grip starts like this. Hold the putter in your right hand down on the bottom of the grip, with your thumb straight down the top, flat part of the grip (Figure 8.1). Now put the left hand on. Put the putter in the crease of your left palm. The last three fingers of the left hand wrap around the grip, the thumb goes down the top of the grip, and the forefinger points straight down at the ground covering the fingers on the right hand (Figure 8.2). Snug everything together and you have yourself a reverse overlap grip, the grip used by most professional golfers and low handicap golfers (Figure 8.3).

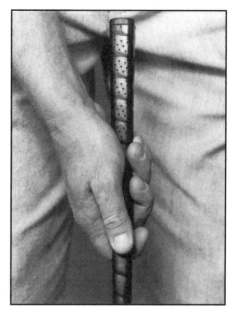

Figure 8.1. The right hand goes on first for the reverse overlap grip.

The cross handed grip puts the hands on reversed of what your normal golf grip would be. You grip the top of the putter grip with your right hand. Again the thumb points down the flat, top part of the putter grip. Now your left hand grips down on the grip under your right hand, thumb pointing down the flat, top part of the grip also (Figure 8.4). You now have a cross hand grip, another effective way to take your hands out of the stroke and improve. Try this one, too and see how it feels. One of the two grips that you just learned will feel better than the other. Whichever one feels better, go with it.

REQUIREMENTS TO PUTT WELL

Did you ever miss a bunch of short putts in a row and wonder what was going on? Chances are you were not fulfilling the three

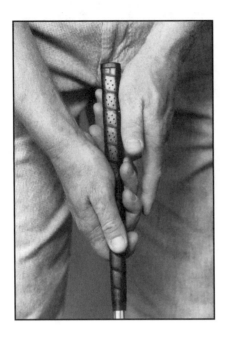

Figure 8.2. The left hand goes on with the forefinger covering the fingers on the right hand.

Figure 8.3. A completed reverse overlap grip.

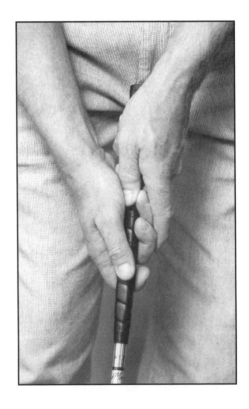

requirements to putt well. It's true that some putts will miss because of a bad read, grain or some influence outside of your control; however, if you get three basics down, you will give yourself the best chance of making any putt.

To putt well, you need to accomplish these three things. Your eyes must be directly over the ball and target line, you need the correct ball position, and you need to use a pure pendulum

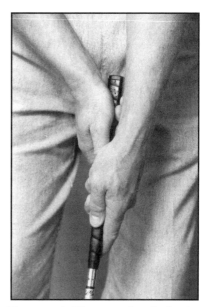

Figure 8.4. The cross handed grip.

stroke in which only your shoulders move, not your hands or wrists. Let's discuss this more in depth.

You must first get your eyes directly over the target line. If your eyes are anywhere but directly over the ball, you're not going to be looking directly down the target line. I rarely see a golfer with his eyes outside the target line. That would mean that the ball is closer to your body than your head, and that would be somewhat uncomfortable. Most often, I see golfers with their eyes on the inside of the target line. That means the ball is too far away from their body. In this position, you are looking down the target line from an angle. The tendency then is to push or more often pull your putt off line to compensate for the angle you are looking from. You may put a beautiful stroke on the ball, but still miss. If your eyes are directly over the line and the ball, you are looking right down the target line. This will give you a clear picture of where you are going, and give you the best chance of rolling the ball right down the target line. Number one is to get your eyes directly over the ball and target line.

The second thing we need to do is get the correct ball position. Find the middle of your stance. The correct ball position is 2" forward toward your left heel from the center of your stance (Figure 8.5). This gives the ball the correct roll. An incorrect ball position will create too much skid or top spin. The other thing a good ball position will do is prevent pushes and pulls. If the ball is too far back in your putting stance, it can result in a push to the right, too far forward will give you a pull. Neither is good. Number two is to have the correct ball position 2" forward of the middle of our stance.

Here is a fun drill to make sure you have your eyes over the

target line and the correct ball position all in one. Put a ball in your left pocket and one on the ground. Address the ball on the ground with your correct putter set up. Without changing your set up, reach into your pocket with your left hand and get your other ball out. Hold it to your left temple and drop it. If it hits the other ball on the ground, your eyes and ball position are correct (Figure 8.6). This is a very informative drill and will tell you a lot about

Figure 8.5. Ball position for putting is 2" forward of center in your stance.

your set up. That is why you see tour professionals doing this drill. A fun way to check your set up.

We have our eyes over the ball and a good ball position. The third thing we need to do is stroke the ball with a pendulum stroke in which our shoulders are the only part of us that moves. Let's back track a little. I love to trick my students by asking them this question "What is more important in putting, distance or direction?" Almost without exception, the class will shout "direction." The reasoning is if you don't get it on the right line, it can't go in. True, but distance is far more critical. Here's why. If I get a putt on perfect line, but come up three feet long or short, I still have a three footer left. If I miss read the putt by three inches, but get the speed right,

I have a three-inch putt left. I'll take the three inches, thanks. Think about it for a moment. When you 3 or 4 putt it's generally distance that you are blowing, not the line. Sure, we all miss a short putt now and again, but if you 3 putt, you didn't get your first putt close enough to tap in.

So we have established distance as a critical factor for getting more balls to drop in the hole, or at least

Figure 8.6. If your ball hits the other ball, your ball position and set up are correct.

get close enough to tap in. That's where the shoulder-only motion comes in. This also ties in with our grip. Both take the wrists out of our motion, which is what we are seeking. Our wrists stay still. If they move during our putting stroke, we have acceleration that we not only don't need, but we don't want either. It's easier to control one source of acceleration, the key word being control.

Grab your putter and do this drill. Take a few strokes without a ball. See if your wrists move. If they do, start to practice not moving them. Just watch them as you take practice strokes and make sure they don't break down (Figure 8.7). If you would like a teaching aid to help you, here is an inexpensive one. Get a plastic ruler and slip it behind your wristwatch when you are practicing your putting. If your left wrist tries to break down, the ruler will stop it. This is a fun drill using an ordinary item. Since putting is such an important part of the game, there are many teaching aids on the market. Most of them work very well. I think that if they help you reinforce the three basic fundementals and are not very expensive, then go for it. What many of the training aids get you to do is something you

Figure 8.7. Firm waists are a must for a great putting stroke.

should do anyway, which is practice. Once you get a good stroke, there is no substitute for stroking a few every day to retain the feel, even if it's on the rug in your home or office. While you do, use your ruler to keep your wrists from breaking down.

With our wrists solid, we have a one-lever stroke that will give us consistency in the distance we hit the ball. If we bring the wrists into the stroke, we are bound to get some surprises. Like when you have a ten-foot putt, miss it, and then have a seven footer coming back. We added something to that stroke that shouldn't have been there. The putting stroke is as simple a motion as there is. Only your shoulders move. We should not complicate it.

I never liked the thought of matching a back swing length to a certain length putt. This was popular a few years back, but in my estimation it replaces feel with a mechanical thought. How can we develop any feel if we are thinking, "Let's see, a ten-foot putt, that means I need to take the putter back ten inches?" Not a good idea. I can't imagine anyone possibly being able to effectively figure that out every time. The game has been dissected to pieces anyway, so let's not take feel out of our putting. I like to demonstrate the concept of feel in this way. I give each of my students a ball and put them at various distances from me. Then one at a time, I ask them to toss the ball to me. No one ever throws it over my head or into the ground in front of me. Then I ask how they figured out how hard to throw it? Did any of them say "It's a five-yard throw, so I have to take my arm back one foot?" Of course not. They knew how hard to throw it by feel, and they developed feel through repetition. Whenever you do anything over and over again, you develop feel. Feel for putting distance is something no one can teach you, it can only be learned by practice. Feel is up to you.

Our back swing should be shorter than our forward swing, period. This will prevent deceleration (a common cause of stubbing), and ensure an accelerating stroke. Take out your putter and with firm wrists stroke it across the ground in a putting motion. Go short back and through, short back and through. Keep your body very steady and move only your shoulders.

There are a zillion putting stances, and most of them are effective. I like to drop my left foot off the target line a little, a slightly open stance. Make sure your shoulders are square to the target line. Get comfortable on your feet. Some players like to point their toes in, pigeon toed. Some like them flared out and others find open or closed comfortable. As long as your shoulders are square to the target, your ball position is correct, and your eyes are directly over the ball, the rest is up to you.

FINDING THE RIGHT PUTTER FOR YOU

Now that we have a good set up, let's look at our equipment. Now that you know how you should be standing, get your putter and set up to it. Do you feel comfortable standing over it? Is it too long, so that the handle catches in your jacket? Is it too short so that you feel too bent over and it makes your back sore? Remember, if your putter doesn't fit, you will not like to practice with it, so get a length that you feel comfortable standing over. There is something funny about the world of putter sales. Even though the putter has to work for you, as soon as someone on tour wins with a certain putter, everyone goes and buys one, as if it will do the same for them. Do you practice putting three hours a day, five days a week? Then these magical putters sell for astronomical prices. I saw a four hundred dollar putter in a magazine today. FOUR HUNDRED

DOLLARS FOR A PUTTER! For that price, I expect the tour player who won with it to come over and putt for me when I play.

I recommend that you find a putter that fits you, is of good quality, is reasonably priced, and looks good to you when you stand over it. It should have some kind of alignment aid on it. Stainless steel and brass have good feel, as do copper. Get a head design that you like to look at. Normally, mallet heads are good on slower greens, and blades or heel toe weighted putters work well on fast greens. That is being very general, however, as I personally know exceptions to that rule.

Shop around. Ask to try a putter that you are interested in on a real green if you can. Since you don't beat on a putter, this should not be a problem. Most shops will let you take a putter out to try if you leave a credit card blank with them. The greens inside shops are generally fine to feel a putter's performance when you can't take it outside. If you feel comfortable over it, and you make some putts, get it.

Now the kicker. Regardless of how many putters you have in your collection, stick with the same one all the time when you play. It should become your scoring partner. Know it like the back of your hand. As any professional will tell you, it's not the putter, it's the puttee. When you are stroking the ball well, you could putt with a 2 x 4. If a putter works well one day, then goes dead, golfers somehow think the molecular structure of the metal changed or something. I don't think so. I somehow think the culprit is the person holding the putter. Something changes in our set up or stroke.

But now that we know the three things that we must do well to putt well, we should be able to correct ourselves. By the way, does this mean that your putter collection just rusts away in your garage? No, that should not happen. We should look at those as vintage cars. They were retired because they could not provide reliable transportation, but they're still fun to play with once in a while. Take your old putters for a spin when you are practicing occasionally, sometimes a different perspective can help your stroke. But use your primary putter for everyday transportation.

I have an old Taylor Made blade that I have been using forever. We get along quite well, just because we've been friends so long. I have a mallet with all kinds of lines on it that I practice with once in a while. I think it makes me appreciate the simplicity of my blade. The blade never lies, if I hit it well, it goes in. If I hit it bad, well, you know the rest. Become good friends with your putter and treat it nicely. You will be hitting that more than any other club, so you should know each other well.

I am often asked about the long putters that have become popular with some senior tour players, on whether they work or not. First of all, if you have any back problems, I think these would be very friendly on your back and allow you to practice more. If it gets you on the practice green more you are bound to become a better putter and I'm all for that.

The other condition the long putter can correct is someone who breaks their wrists and can't stop. I run into a student every once in a while who simply struggles with keeping the wrists still during the putting stroke. No matter how much they try or practice, when they get over a putt on the course, BAM, their wrists break down and no one knows where the ball is going. I would never fault someone for that happening, it just happens. So if there is a way to correct it, and help them get the ball in the hole, again I'm all for it.

How the long putters work is you anchor the top grip against your chest with the left hand, and lightly hold the other grip with the right hand. There are a few different ways to hold on with the right hand, but generally the right index finger points down the grip. With only one hand actually on the club, there is no pivot point to break down. It swings like a pendulum on a clock. My students tell me that they feel the long putters are easily as accurate, if not more so, on the short putts inside six feet. The longer putts are slightly more difficult, but I'm sure with practice you could get the hang of it. They are not for everyone, but if you need to use one, don't hold back, just get good with it.

DISTANCE DRILL

Here is a good way to practice distance. The zig-zag drill will help you develop the feel you need to handle any putt you come up against. Go to the putting green with six balls. Lay a ball one foot from the hole, and add three feet to each ball you lay down in a zig-zag pattern (Figure 8.8). The first ball is one foot away, the second four feet, the third seven feet and so on. You zig-zag so that you don't get used to a certain break. Since we want to be able to two putt from any-where on the green, par for

Figure 8.8. The zig-zag drill.

these six balls is 12. You may say "Jim, the first ball is only a foot away." You've never missed one of those? O.K., I didn't think so. Anyway, putt the closest one first, the second closest one second and so on. Hole each ball before going on to the next one. When you finish, add your score and see how you did. As you get better, separate the balls farther, so number six is 30 or 40 feet away. Always put the first ball at one to two feet away.

When I practice my putting, I set a goal for myself. I may say, "When I get all these balls in on nine strokes, I'm done." Sometimes it takes me an hour, then I know I needed the practice. Sometimes I do it on the first try. If that happens, I quit. I have met the goal I set out to accomplish, and I also know my stroke is good. If it ain't broke, don't fix it. The zig-zag drill is my favorite to practice putting with a purpose. I like it because you have a different putt every putt, just like the golf course. I don't know about you, but when I am on the course, my friends never let me putt a whole pile until I figure out the break and speed. No sir, they only give me one shot, so I like my practice to simulate that, although you can't simulate them hoping you miss.

A PRESHOT ROUTINE TO AIM YOUR PUTT

We know how important distance is, what about direction? That's important also, but once you learn how to aim, distance becomes your focus once again. How do you aim? That is one of the best tricks of the trade. Did you ever notice how deliberate the professionals on television are when they are marking their ball? That's because they are aiming it by pointing the name in the direction that they want the ball to start in. We will incorporate aiming our ball into our preshot routine. Just like all of our other shots, we need to get into the same routine each time we take a putt. As you approach the green, start looking at which way the green tilts so you have a general idea what the putt is going to do. Then start into your preshot routine. Here's how you do it.

1) Take a coin or ball marker and mark your ball by laying the marker directly behind the ball. Pick up your ball and clean it off. A clean ball rolls better.

2) After eyeing up your putt and deciding which direction you want the putt to START, replace the ball where it is marked with the name pointing down the line you want the putt to start on. If it curls to the left, aim right. If it curls to the right, aim left. Your ball is now aimed.

3) Now we can get back to the task at hand which is to hit this putt the correct distance. Take a practice stroke or two from behind the ball looking at the hole (Figure 8.9). Now when you put the putter behind the ball to address it, make sure the alignment line on top of the putter is a square continuation of the name on the ball that you aimed. Take one look back at the hole and pull the trigger.

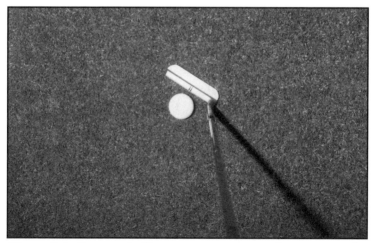

Figure 8.9. Square the line on your putter to the name on the ball after you take a practice stroke.

You will know if the putter was square to the ball by the way it rolls. If you see the name rolling perfectly end over end, then you got it right. If it wobbles, we didn't hit it squarely. This aiming thing takes a bit of practice, but I have never shown this to a golfer who, after working on it a while, didn't make more putts. It's like legal cheating. We can aim our ball. What a game, what a country.

BREAKING PUTTS

How do you read the break on a green? This has always been a touchy subject. It comes down to experience and feel, but here are some helpful tips that I like to share with my students. Suppose I have a putt that is going to break to the left, and it seems pretty obvious. I will get down low and look at this putt from both sides. I will not make any comments to myself like, "eight inches right fast speed." I let feel take over. There is only three results that are possible and after I putt this ball, I will watch and see which result occurred. If I do this enough times, I will start to acquire the experience needed to make a decision on the line and speed of breaking putts.

The three options are 1) It can go in. 2) It can miss on the pro side or, 3) it can miss on the amateur side. On this putt, the pro side is the right or uphill side. The reason this is called the pro side is that if I miss it on the high or "pro" side, it had a chance of falling in. If I missed it on the amateur side or low side, it never had a chance. I like to hit my putts higher up the hill and slower so they die into the hole. If you get too aggressive on putts like this and miss, you can roll it down the hill and leave yourself a tough putt coming back. Remember, distance is everything. There is no exact formula for breaking putts, but we can use some common sense. If we are missing putts on the amateur side often, play for more break.

Another putt that gives golfers a lot of trouble is when we have a big hill between us and the hole. I always try to break this putt into two different putts, the one that I do and the one that the hill does. I will look at the hill and decide where I would have to place the ball if it were to simply roll down the hill under its own power and go in the hole. Then I figure out how I have to hit my putt to get it to that point rolling slowly. I then forget the hole and focus on the spot that I'm putting to. Again, speed is everything. It's all about feel and experience and common sense. I'll bet I don't have to tell you to hit uphill putts harder and downhill putts softer. I didn't think so. If you can find a practice green with some undulation it will help.

When you practice severely breaking putts, don't be too intense. Just watch what the ball does, develop feel, try to 2 putt all of them, and have fun. It is fascinating to watch a breaking putt develop after it leaves your putter, but we must be observant. Breaking putts are very rewarding when you start to develop the feel for getting them close, so enjoy them and learn from each one you putt.

SHORT PUTTS

The only putt that is guaranteed to go in is one that's already in the bottom of the cup. If I go through my preshot routine and take every putt seriously, the short putts have a pretty good chance of going in. If I get complacent and just take a swat at a two footer, I'm not giving myself the best chance possible of making that putt. Take it from me, that short putt deserves as much focus as a 240 yard drive. You wouldn't get up on the tee and lean over, not really look at your target, take no practice swing, and take an off-balance stab at your ball with a driver, would you? That sounds ridiculous, but that is basically what we are doing when we take those short putts for granted. If we don't prepare well, we can't expect a good result. When I play in a tournament, I am very deliberate with my preshot routine and the results on the short putts are generally good. If I do miss one, I know that I gave it my best shot. Then comes social golf, and even I am not immune to stupidity. At least once every two months or so, I am playing along nicely and take a short putt for granted, stab at it and miss. I feel so dumb when I do that, knowing that I just absolutely wasted a stroke. Then I am really focused for another couple of months until I remind myself again with another random act of brainlessness. I think it's human nature, we see the tour professionals do that occasionally too. Isn't it good to know that you are not alone?

There is something else that can affect your short putting. That is the "gimme," and here is the problem. In match play, when one side concedes a putt to the other side, they must accept. In match play the game is played one hole at a time, with one player or team winning or losing each hole. In stroke play, you are playing for total score for your 18 holes, and the player or team with the lowest score wins. If you are playing match play, which is rare, and you concede your opponent's putt, he must pick it up. When would you do this? If he hits it to 3" from the hole for birdie, and you are 10 feet and must make it for birdie, the nice thing to do is concede his putt. He has hit a brilliant shot, and you should have to work to tie or "half" the hole.

The point I'm making is that when you are playing, there is no such thing as a "gimme." Every putt must be holed, yet you always hear "that's good." Then it gets farther and farther away that they are considered "good." Soon six footers are "gimmes" and no one knows how to make a two-foot putt. What happens next is the real problem. You get invited to play somewhere as a guest of someone who does not give "gimmes." Next thing you know, you shoot the worst round of your life and say, "I never missed so many short putts in all my life." Is it any wonder? You haven't putted anything under six feet in two years. "Gimmes" also give you a false sense of security in your game. You think that you are a 15 handicap, but that is only until you get up to "inside the leather." From there, you don't even know how you would fare.

The best way to combat this is to agree on the first tee to hole every thing out. I am bound as a P.G.A. professional to remind you that if you all agree to give "gimmes," you have breached rule 1-3 and are all disqualified. Since I can't remember the last time I saw a group disqualify themselves, we will move on. I just thought I'd throw that in to cover myself. Anyway, if the other players don't want to hole all their putts, you do it anyway. After a few holes, they will feel guilty and join you in holing out every putt. It will be much better for everyone. When you say "I shot 87," you will have real satisfaction knowing you really did.

Since we are on the short putt thought, here is a neat drill to practice. Address a ball that is about one foot from the hole, then close your eyes and putt it, listening for it to go into the hole. Eventually extend these to three feet away and try it, keeping your eyes closed when you stroke. Feel will take over. What a super drill for not only keeping your eyes down during the stroke, but building the confidence needed to make the short ones. I also like to practice three footers in a circle. Again, it's lots of fun and builds loads of confidence. I put eight balls in a three-foot circle around the hole and work my way around. If I miss one, I have to start again. Sometimes on the first go around I will sink them all. If that happens, I go on to something else and retain the confidence that I'm great from three feet.

Make sure that your putting practice is fun and goal oriented. Set your goals and when you accomplish them, move on to something else. If you were to reach a particular goal, and do more of the same drill, it will lose its appeal and you will probably lose your intensity. If you can practice with someone, that can up the fun factor considerably. I love to practice with my dad. Not only do we get in some good practice, but we also get some quality time together, which is what golf is truly about. Nothing better than sharing a common interest with people you enjoy.

So there are three fundamentals that must be met to putt well. We must have our eyes directly over the ball and target line, the ball position must be 2" forward of the center of our stance, and we should use a pure pendulum stroke where the wrists stay firm. Only our shoulders should be moving. Aim the ball using the name and use the same preshot routine every time you putt for consistency. The key in your practice is to get a feel for distance.

TO SUM IT UP

To sum it up, our short game develops in three stages, practice, feel, and imagination. First, we need to learn the mechanics of a good short game, which I have spelled out for you in the preceding pages. Keep it simple. I would rather you be great at a few shots than have fifty different shots in your bag, none of which work well. Get the mechanics down and practice these shots until we can count on them to work consistently. At that point we begin to develop feel, our second stage. How do we know when we are there? Feel starts to show itself when you have a 30-yard pitch and you put it to five feet, and on the next hole you have a eight-yard chip and put it to one foot. You will look back and remember when the first shot would have come up short of the green and the second one would have rolled way past the hole. After you have become mechanically sound and have developed some feel, something neat happens. You begin to use imagination on shots. You start to see shots that you would not have envisioned before. The place where you unsuccessfully bladed a pitching wedge last year you brilliantly use an 8 iron chip this year. You are suddenly disappointed if your putt from 20 feet lips out, when months ago you could have 4 putted from there. You are down right speechless because you missed a putt on the amateur side.

Develop and let your short game grow. Be fearless and show the long hitters how to score.

Let's Practice, Let's Play

I n this chapter I am going to give you tips on playing, practicing, course management, picking the right club, and mentally preparing yourself, among other subjects. It is intended to help you play the game better and have more fun. Golf is always a challenge, but it's a lot more fun if you are playing well and feel somewhat in control. I don't know of a worse feeling on the golf course than spiraling out of control and not being able to get back on track. We will realize that a preshot routine is of tremendous value when the wheels start falling off. We can learn to self-correct to a certain extent. If we have a general idea what is happening with our swing, we don't have to continue playing a swing fault that jumps up in the middle of a round. We can learn how to dismantle a hole and play smartly to our strong suit, not shoot from the hip, and hope for the best. Let's get started.

THE PRACTICE RANGE

Our first stop is the driving range, the place where we work on the mechanical aspects of our swing. We play golf on the golf course, and practice on a range. On the golf course, our only goal is to get the ball into the hole in the least amount of strokes. On the driving range, the object is to hone the mechanical skills required to be able to get the ball in the hole on the course. Note that on the course we want a minimum of mechanical thoughts, on the range we can ponder the physical movements we make and assess their effectiveness. Keep those two goals distinctly separate, unless you are working on course management or trying out something that you have been practicing during a practice round on the course.

We need to use our time wisely on the range. At least 50% of your practice time should be spent on the short game. I see it all the time at the range. People hitting driver after driver while the putting green is empty. Granted it's more fun to hit drivers and other long shots, but it's infinitely more fun to lower your score 10 strokes consistently because you have been practicing your short game too. If you live in a seasonal area, on the off season you should have a putting rug in your house. More strokes saved in the spring.

So how can you practice effectively at the range? Here is a good plan to use. If it is only a general practice session, after warming up, start with a pitching wedge and take 10 shots, each progressively farther than the one before. You must know where you are aimed, so look down the corner of the mat or lay a club on the ground for alignment. Then hit five shots with the 8 iron, five shots with the 6 iron ,and five shots with the 4 iron. Then hit five shots with a fairway wood, and five with the driver. Here's where most golfers make a big mistake. They will then begin pounding drivers until their tempo is shot and confidence broken. You never hit 30 drivers in three minutes on the golf course, yet most folks think they can on the range. Your long clubs demand loads of concentration, and you can't do that if you're hitting them like a machine gun. Hit five good drivers or the biggest club in your bag, and then work your way down the bag, hitting the ones that you missed on the way up, 3, 5, 7, and 9. Finish up with a few sand wedges, and then go off to where you can pitch,chip and putt. That's for a good all-around tune-up session.

Sometimes you need to work on a particular club. If it happens to be your driving club, fight the urge to just get up and start ripping at it. Your tempo will suffer, as you will probably start off swinging way too fast. Hit some wedges and 7 irons before you hit your driving club. Then, to slow yourself down, hit five of the drives, and five of the 7 irons, then five drives and five pitching wedges and so on. This will keep you at a good pace, smooth and slow. The worst thing you can do is bring only a driver and hit a whole bucket with it. You will only wear yourself out and waste your time.

There is a very common phenomenon that afflicts many golfers. It's called, "I hit it perfect on the range, but sideways on the course" syndrome. Do you suffer from this? The symptoms are as follows. You can swing free and easy on the range, loose as a goose and feeling good. Driver?, no problem, where do you want me to put it? Pitching wedge, ten in a row within ten feet. Then you get to the course. After slicing your first drive into the next county, you're standing on the second tee three over par wondering where the sweet swinging machine that just gave a clinic on the range went. It can happen to us all, but it is curable with a good preshot routine. I'll explain.

THE PRESHOT ROUTINE

There is a definite difference between the range and the golf course. The first difference you notice on the course is that you only get one shot at it. You are not allowed to carry a whole bucket of balls and keep hitting each shot until it goes the way you want. Difference number two is the fact that all of a sudden on the course you are forced to play within certain parameters. The first hole has water on the left and out of bounds on the right. I don' t remember seeing anything like that on the range, and even if there were, I didn't care. I wasn't going to be penalized if I hit it. No, I would just reach down and get another ball. Now I am on the course and it just cost me $9.00 in lost balls on the last three holes. Lastly, other people on the range never stopped to watch me hit, but now even the squirrels are making me nervous watching me. Does this sound familiar?

As I was growing as a golfer something happened that helped me as much as anything I learned throughout my career. I was playing with a professional that I had and still have great respect for. I would carefully set up to the ball, swing, hear a perfect click, and knowing that I had just hit a great shot look up to see my ball going into a bunker or somewhere that I didn't want it to go. When we got done, he said, "Jim, you have a beautiful swing, we only need to apply it to the target line." He then proceeded to teach me a basic preshot routine, which I have developed over the years into a routine for my students that will allow them to transpose their range swing onto the golf course.

If you look at the professionals on the tours, it's their preshot routine that they hide in when they are in pressure situations. If you learn a good preshot routine, and use it faithfully, it is like a good friend that stays with you on every shot. It also allows you to line up correctly and get into the same position every time you hit. All good golfers use one. Many senior golfers that I teach never learned a preshot routine and when they do it changes their game. Another benefit is that when you are getting into the same position each time, it's easier to detect a problem or identify something wacky in your ball flight. By the way, we will practice this at the driving range as intensely as any other part of our game.

A good preshot routine will let you enjoy the game much more. Do you come home from the golf course feeling like you just got beat up? Often this has to do with your ability to go in and out of different concentration levels during a round. Golf is not a four-hour marathon of headache-producing concentration. It is a series of 30-second periods of concentration, with the rest of the time in between to be spent enjoying the great outdoors or the company of your friends. A preshot routine will allow you to separate yourself from your game in between shots, so you can stop and smell the roses. Then when it's time to hit again, you can enter the concentration zone, with your preshot routine being your key to get in.

When I was at a local P.G.A. seminar a few years ago, I saw something that was fascinating. The speaker was a noted sports psychologist and showed us the results of a brain wave test done on a tour pro during a tournament round. In between shots there was very little activity, indicating someone not particularly focused on anything. As he approached his ball, activity increased and was clearly represented by a rise in the graph on the chart. The graph steadily rose until it was its highest at impact. Then it declined rapidly back down to the minimal level. This graphically reinforced the importance of the preshot routine. When you learn to repeat it consistently, you no longer fish around for the right positions. They come naturally since you have done them so many times before. Then you can have fun in between shots.

Here is the preshot routine that I recommend. Do you remember in the grip chapter that we now get our grip with the club up in the air? Now we will find out why that is so important. To practice our first preshot routines, we will use a 7 iron. We will learn later in this chapter how to choose the right club for a particular shot.

1) Stand behind the ball and make an imaginary line between the ball and your target. You may use an interim target,(a leaf or spot on the ground) if it is on the same target line. Make sure you hit square to the mat or have a club pointed down the target so we know where we are aimed. Obviously we won't be laying clubs down on the golf course, but we will do that on the range until we have a clear understanding of where square is and how to get there.

2) Get your grip with the club in the air. Make sure the lines on the club face are straight up and down (perpendicular to the ground). Can you see two knuckles on your left hand? Softly extend your arms.

3) Looking at the target line or interim target, place the club on the ground square (perpendicular) to the target line.

4) Put your feet together. This next step is important. With your feet close together, measure yourself to the ball. You should be on the balls of your feet and feel springy. At this point you should measure one hand width from the butt of the club to your left leg (Figure 9.1).

5) Now as we separate our feet, we need to get the correct ball position. I always move my left foot first, according to what club I'm playing. If I am playing a driver, and need a ball position even with my left big toe, I simply flare my left foot without moving it to the left, then move my right foot to shoulder width. If I am playing a pitching wedge, I will move my left foot, flare it out, and then move my right foot so that the ball position is in the middle of my stance. All of the other clubs I adjust accordingly to the correct ball

Figure 9.1. Feet together, springy, and one hand width from the club to your leg.

position, this requires a little practice and awareness on your part, but is well worth it.

6) Since your body naturally aligns your shoulders a little open, and we want them square to the target line, this is when I twist my shoulders slightly to the right to square them up. Now we can relax, take one last look back to the target, and pull the trigger.

I know what you are thinking. It's going to take ten minutes to do all of that. The first time, maybe you are right. When I learned the preshot routine, it took a long time at first, but I was so convinced it would help me that I practice it faithfully on every ball I hit for five buckets of balls. By the time I got to the fifth bucket, I had the whole routine down to about 20 seconds. I was thrilled to find that I hit more quality shots and they went where I wanted them to go much more often than before. This took my game to the next level. On the golf course I felt I could now spend more focus on playing the game, not fishing around for the correct mechanics each swing.

There is a psychological point I would like to make about preshot routine before we go on. Many of the people who play golf are dynamic personalities. There are exceptions, but for the most part they are doers. They like to do things. They also are often organized, thinking people. A preshot routine brings some sanity to an otherwise very inconsistent undertaking. To a certain extent, we are used to being at least somewhat in control of our surroundings. The fact that we so often feel out of control on the golf course drives us nuts. We like to have things organized and categorized. A preshot routine is something in golf that we can have total control over all of the time, on every shot we take. It gives you a fighting chance. Once you get it down, you will never feel comfortable taking a shot again without doing it.

Once again, I can use my father as an example of what a preshot routine can do for your game. Here is a man who was an educator his entire life. Although not a golf instructor, he was prepared and organized every day of his life. Then dad retired and took up the game seriously. He loves the game, the exercise, and the fact that you must think to play well. The only thing he didn't like is the lack of organization in his own game. Dad likes to prepare well and reap the benefits of good preparation. Enter the preshot routine. The perfect way for dad to get organized before each shot. He saw a dramatic change in the way he approached each shot and so will you. Now he gives himself the best chance at success when he goes through his preshot routine.

Golfers sometimes think that a preshot routine will slow play. The fact is, you will hit so many more quality shots that it will actually save time. Did you ever rush a shot because there were people behind you? Or my favorite example is when golfers want you to play through, which is a pressure-filled situation that you need help focusing. The first tee is another good example of a place that a preshot routine can help you focus. These are very exciting situations, and people really appreciate a good shot when you hit one. If you use your preshot routine, it takes your mind off of everything except the task at hand. You will become much less nervous in those situations, and be able to perform well with others watching.

Speaking of nerves, I would like to share some thoughts that I have realized along my golfing journey. Nervous is a negative word. You are excited, not nervous. Being excited is positive, and that's good. Always remember that. It is an honor to be on a golf course. There are places in the world where they have never heard the word golf. You could have been born there. Always remember that, too. Pressure in golf is all self-imposed. If you see someone hit a bad shot, you show empathy. You say, "Oh man, tough break" or something like that. You don't say, "That #%$%$¢¢ idiot is the worst golfer in the world and should have his clubs taken away !!!" Yet we think when we hit a bad shot, everyone is thinking the same thing. I am a P.G.A professional, but some of my most fun rounds have been with high handicappers. I judge you by who you are, not how you shoot. I think we all do, until we are the one who hits the bad shot. Don't worry about it, we all chop it once in a while. Our objective is to chop it less often than we did in the past. He or she who chops the least, wins.

So we have worked on our swing and it feels good. We have done our preshot routine on the range many times until we feel we have it down. There is another wonderful drill we can do at the driving range that will help us prepare for the course. I call it a drill, but it really is a fun game to make the most of your practice.

We know that it's hard to transpose our range swing on to the course. We can practice at the range just like it's the course. Here's how. Take out a driving wood, 5 iron, 8 iron and pitching wedge, or the combination that you have closest to those clubs. This is fun to do with someone, but you can do it alone. First, you need to set parameters. You may say that for your tee shots to be in play, they must be between the 150-yard sign and the maintenance shed, or whatever you have on your range that you can use for reference. Then you would do the same for your five iron. Perhaps the target green at the 150-yard mark or something similar. Pick a target for your 8 iron, and one for the wedge. Also pick a target to pitch or chip to.

You can make a total of five points per "hole," one point for each shot that falls at the target and one for a good pitch or chip. Taking turns, each "Player" hits a tee shot and whoever gets one in the "fairway" makes a point. Then do the same with 5 iron, 8 iron, and pitching wedge. For the fifth shot, you pitch or chip to a target. Do this rotation 18 times. If both players are of similar skill levels, then you can add up your points and whoever gets the most wins. If you are at different levels, you can either make the parameters harder for the better player, or use a match play format, where there is a winner each "hole." Anyway you do it, it's fun.

I like everything about this drill. It slows you down and makes you use your preshot routine on each shot. It simulates real course pressure, because you only get one shot with each club at a time. This way, you learn to change from club to club easily. It will create some good friendly competition instead of aimlessly beating balls with no purpose. In addition, this drill will tell you exactly what parts of your game are working and which need work. Whoever loses, buys coffee on the way home. Now we will go to the golf course and see if we can improve our performance.

PLAYING THE GAME: PICK THE RIGHT TEES

Do you play a course that fits your skill level? Do you play the correct tees when you go to different courses? Do you play with good friends, or do you play with people better than yourself who try to intimidate you into playing a course or tees that are above your skill level? We need to address this, especially as seniors if we are to enjoy the game the way it should be.

The first thing you need to do is honestly identify your skill level. When I used to go snow skiing with my friends, there was always someone who would talk us into skiing the expert slopes. We were good skiers, but not experts. So under the constant fear of a horrible death, we would crawl down the expert slope, one turn at a time. It was not fun. It was also the place I formulated my philosophy for future endeavors. I would rather be an expert on intermediate slopes, than an intermediate on the expert slopes. You will not be physically injured playing a golf course that is too hard for you, but we have all experienced that slow 18-hole demise, playing a course that was way too hard for our skill level.

If you belong to a club, look at the yardage from the different tees. If you and your senior friends who play all the time have difficulty reaching the holes in regulation, ask the professional if they will put in a set of senior tee markers. Here in Florida many courses are going to that. It's the right thing to do. You should be having fun. Not being able to reach any of the holes in regulation can get old real fast. The professional should oblige, as they are there to make the game better for you. I am not talking about building new tees. Simply get a new color tee marker and put them in the back of the front tee box. If your course uses a long continual tee box, move them up just behind the ladies and in front of the white tees so everyone can have fun.

Realize that I am also not saying to make the course so short that it is not a challenge. I know of no other action sport that 70 year olds are expected to compete on the same level of 25 year olds. Even if your strength has diminished, you should still be rewarded with a well-struck shot to the green. I have never believed that you should be penalized for not hitting the ball as far as you once did.

Here's what I do with my dad. I play the back tees and he plays the "senior" tees. If we play somewhere that does not have senior tees, I look at the yardage of the course. If it is too heavy from the white tees, I insist he plays from the red or front tees. He strikes the ball beautifully, but doesn't hit it as far as he once did. From those respective tees, if I hit driver and he hits driver proportionally well, we both have maybe 6 irons into the green, mine from 165 yards, his from 135 yards. What's the big deal?; you still have to hit a great shot to score well. This keeps the game interesting, we can have a match that measures talent, and dad can have fun, too, instead of hitting 3 wood into every green.

In case you are wondering, the courses they play on the senior tour are significantly shorter than the ones they play on the regular tour. Spectators want to see birdies, not guys hitting 2 iron into the greens. You will also notice new courses, especially resorts, building five different tee boxes and assigning handicap recommendations to each one. Take a particular par 3 hole. The tees may be built as follows; back tees 203 yards, blue tees 176 yards, white tees 154 yards, gold tees 128 yards, red tees 108 yards. Everyone can find a tee box that suits his or her game. In this particular situation, I would have dad play off the white or gold tees, depending on the yardage of the rest of the holes. From the back tee, it's a 3 iron for me. From the whites, it's a 4 iron for dad. I should say that would even things up a bit. This speeds play and ensures that everyone has a good time. What a great idea.

Since there will be golfers of many different skill levels reading this book, this next point is worth mentioning. If you are a newer golfer, try to find a course that fits your skill level, then graduate to bigger courses. Even a full-length course that has different tee boxes can be too much for you. The executive style or par 3 courses offer a fun alternative to the full-length championship courses.

In the area my school is located, there are many manufactured home communities that have executive courses winding through them. They maintain a tremendous level of activity, and everyone seems to be having a ball. It may have to do with the fact that the course is not overwhelming to ladies and beginners, and the long hitters have no advantage. Obviously, if you are a long hitter, this would probably not give you enough challenge.

You are the only one who can decide what type of course you should play. Just make sure to play a course that you can have fun playing. There is no shame to having fun and that's why they build so many different kinds of courses.

Can a professional or low handicap player have fun on a short par 3 or executive course? Yes! The par 3 courses usually have very small greens and plenty of challenge. It's a great place for the better player to sharpen up his short game. I just make believe that the tee box is where my normal drive would land on a full-length course. Then it's like I am hitting my shot on to the green of a par 4. This is a super way to practice everything except your woods.

PRE HANDICAP YOUR SCORECARD

Want another way to take some pressure off yourself on the golf course? Pre handicap your score card. Here is how it works. First, you need to know what your handicap is. If you belong to a club, then you probably know already. If you don't belong to a club, you can have your handicap maintained at one of the public courses in the area that offer handicap service. It normally only costs a few dollars, and they will provide you with a current handicap card showing your handicap. For you newer golfers, your handicap is the average number of strokes above par that you shoot in a round of golf. Loosely translated, if par on a golf course is 72 and you are an 18 handicap, your average score is 90. Let's use dad as an example again.

When we used to play, dad would put too much pressure on himself trying to make par on every hole, not a very realistic goal for an 18 handicap. What I started doing is pre handicapping his card. The first thing you do is draw a diagonal line across each box that you put your hole by hole score in. Then in the top half of each box, put par plus your handicap stroke. In Figure 9.2, I have added dad's one stroke per hole to par. On the first hole, it's a par 4, but a par 5 for dad according to his handicap. This way, when he looks at each hole, it looks a lot more reasonable than looking for par all the time. When he does make a par, it feels like a birdie and builds his confidence. If he makes a double bogey, it feels like a bogey and doesn't feel so bad. One thing is for sure, he has played better since doing this. That I like.

It was easy to do with an 18 handicap, but what if you are a 28 handicap. You would get one stroke on all holes, and two strokes on the ten hardest holes. How do we know what the ten hardest holes are? On every score card is a handicap rating of each hole, with one

HOLE	1	2	3	4	5	6	7	8	9	OUT	10	11	12	13	14	15	16	17	18	IN	Tot	Hcp	Net
BLUE / 0-8 HDCP 70.7/118	363	412	201	385	416	331	508	201	502	3319	455	474	148	382	540	184	391	370	432	3376	6695		
WHITE / 9-24 HDCP 69.1/115	339	403	189	368	405	310	495	148	474	3131	441	460	138	369	499	173	374	355	409	3218	6349		
RED / 25+ HDCP 72.1/119	322	398	180	354	348	244	455	115	417	2833	408	420	97	359	411	165	358	319	333	2870	5703		
MEN'S/LADIES'	13/7	3/3	7/15	5/13	1/1	17/11	11/5	9/17	15/9		2/2	16/14	18/18	10/12	14/16	12/8	8/10	6/6	4/4				
HARRY · 18 HDCP	5	4	3	5	5	6	4	6	45		5	6	4	5	6	4	5	5	5	45	90		
JOE · 28 HDCP	6	5	6	6	5	6	5	6	50		6	6	4	6	6	4	6	6	6	50	100		
PAR MEN'S/LADIES'	4	4/5	3	4	4	4	5	3	5	36/37	4/5	5	3	4	5	3	4	4	4	36/37	72/74		

Figure 9.2. Harry is an 18 handicap, Joe is a 28. This is what a pre handicapped card looks like.

being the hardest hole and 18 being the easiest. So a person with a 28 handicap would have one stroke on every hole and two strokes on handicap holes one through ten. In Figure 9.2, we have also pre handicapped Joe's score with his 28 handicap. Set up your score card this way, and you too will have a reasonable goal to play for.

COURSE MANAGEMENT TIPS

Let's go over some course management tips to help you when you are out playing on the course. The first question is always, "What is course management anyway?" Let's explain that first. Many golfers assume the way to play is hit it as far as you can every time, chase it, and hit it again. That is acceptable when we are beginning golfers. As we grow into better golfers, our swings normally get better from all the work we put in to them. Often, another major part of the game itself gets neglected, that part being course management. Course management can be described as "using the shot you got," and using it effectively to stay out of trouble. Simply put, it's play-ing smartly enough to maximize your potential, and not trying to play like someone you are not. Obviously, this includes using your head as we were discussing earlier and not biting off too much course by playing from the wrong tees. That would be an error that would follow us during the entire round.

Assuming we are playing a course that is challenging but not overwhelming, the first thing we do is pre handicap our score card. Then we can get into the hole by hole course management. When I play a hole, I have a plan. I look at the hole, and dismantle it back-ward to figure what I should hit off the tee. If I haven't played the course before, I get my input from the yardage and pictures on the score card, the granite hole marker that sometimes has a layout of the hole, anything I can visually see, and the handicap number on the score card.

Yardage should be your first determining factor. Have a plan and try to stick to it. My plan is simple. Aside from any extenuating circumstances, it is as follows. A hole 330 yards or shorter, I use a 2 iron off the tee, which I hit out 225 yards, but very consistently. 330 to 370 it's a 1 iron, 370 on up it's a driver. I use driver off the tee on par 5's up to 500 yards, as I may reach them in two shots, otherwise its 2 iron. Longer par 5's. So you are thinking "Jim, that's great for you, Mr. 225 yard 2 iron, but how about us cats who don't hit our driver that far?" You have a handicap, my friend, so you are often not expected to hit it 250 off the tee.

Where so many golfers get in trouble is by biting off too much on their first shot. Instead of playing something controllable off the tee, they play a club they cannot control and hit it into trouble. Then they feel that they are behind, so they get into more trouble by biting off too much on the second shot. Here is a typical scenario. It is a 330-yard hole. Without planning, you think to yourself, "A good drive will put me into position to hit the green with a short iron." In trying to hit it huge, you top it. You can't believe you just did that, so now you are going to make up for it with a 220 yard 3 wood to the green. This one you really rip, but oh no, it's slicing. In the woods you try to punch out, almost making it, but hit another tree. One more punch out, a chip and two putts later you are writing 7 on your score card and wondering why.

If we were to play again in the afternoon, we would have to think of a way to do better. I frequently ask my students what club they could absolutely, positively, hit straight if they had to? Often it is a 4 or 5 iron, maybe a 5 or 7 wood. If on that same 330 shot you hit something 180 off the tee, that would leave you with about 150 left into the green. I am sure you would rather be 150 yards away from the green in the middle of the fairway hitting your second shot, then punching your fourth shot from the woods. That is easily accomplished by picking the club off the tee that gives you the best chance to score and not take penalty strokes.

To get a good plan off the tee, the first thing is to know how far you hit your different long club options, and how accurately they work for you. Then we can look at the length of the par 4's and make a plan of sorts. Suppose you hit driver 200 to 220 yards but sometimes slice it, 3 wood 180 to 200 good most of the time, and 4 iron 160 to 170 very straight. A good plan for you may be 4 iron off the tee on par 4 holes up to 320 yards, 3 wood off the tee on par 4 holes up to 360 yards and par 5's. If it is a par 4 over 360 yards and there are not any major hazards, a driver may be a good choice. You still want to have some fun and challenge yourself, so if you get a shorter par 4, but the fairway is wide without much trouble to the sides, you can try a driver too.

The main point is to know that there are more options than hammering a big stick off every tee and hoping for the best. If you golfers playing the shorter or executive courses think this doesn't apply to you, surprise, it still does. In fact, sometimes it may be more tempting for you to get pulled into making a mistake than if you were playing a longer course.

Take a look at the number one handicap hole on your course. It is number one for a reason. Suppose it is a 180 yard par 3 and you know you can reach it if you whack your longest club; however, there is trouble all around it. Try at least once laying up just short, say 160 yards, and pitch it close to make par. I am sure if you average your score over several rounds, you will find you do much better when you play smarter.

Remember, the little guy in your head who is saying, "C'mon you chicken, go for it" is nowhere to be found when you write a nine on your score card. So my first rule of course management is pick a club to hit off the tee that will get you good distance but will still be in the fairway most of the time.

My second course management rule is, "use the shot you've got," but don't ever play a shot where if it goes straight it will hurt you. Using "the shot you've got" simply means that if your ball has a slight left to right movement to it, you should play it until such time as you can correct it if it bothers you or you enjoy playing it. There is nothing wrong with playing a ball flight that moves a little left to right or right to left. Most professionals "work" the ball on many of the shots they hit. The only thing you must do is allow for the ball flight, and not aim where a straight shot will penalize you.

For instance, suppose you are shooting to a green with the pin on the left side, but there is a water hazard to the left also. Your normal shot goes left to right. If you aim just left of the pin, it will come back and you will be putting for birdie, what a thrill. The only problem is that about then Murphy's law kicks in, you hit it straight, and it goes into the water. Oops! That's not the end of it, though. Now you have got a tough pitch, probably uphill, to a tight pin that is close to the side that you are on, making it difficult to get close. If we go back to that same 7 iron shot and hit it slightly right of the pin, we will be in good shape. If it goes straight by some miracle, all of our friends will congratulate us for hitting it close. If it fades like we assume it will do, we are still safely on the green, taking one or two putts, and going on to our next adventure.

The same rule applies to tee shots. I wish I had a nickel for every time I have observed a golfer carefully line up way left to play his slice, and then proceed to rip the tee shot of his life right into the woods or water. What you must do is aim left enough to allow your shot to come around. If you must aim where if you hit it straight you're dead, drop down a club or two. A shorter club will not have as much action on it because of its back spin. You will be happy as can be in the fairway, while the rest of the group is searching the hazards for their balls. So rule number two is "use the shot you've got," but don't aim to a spot where a straight shot is going to hurt you.

Rule number three is a good one that we can all identify with. As senior golfers, there are going to be times that you will have to swallow your pride and lay up short of water or some other hazard. Try to picture this. You have 190 yards to go to the green, but a pond guards the front of the green. At one time you would have thought about going for it, but now you are going to use your head so you can make par or bogey. You estimate the pond is about half the remaining distance, which would be about 95 yards. You take out your 90-yard club to give yourself some room for error and swing. It is a perfect shot except for the fact that it rolls into the pond at the end of its roll. Right about then you mumble, "nice lay up" to yourself as you stroll in disbelief to the edge of the pond to fish out your ball. Rule number three therefore must be: Lay up well short of trouble. The additional five yards can't help you if three of them are underwater.

This applies to ditches, ponds, creeks, dog legs, and any other situation where too long a shot will put a beating on your score and confidence. If you truly hit a lousy shot, you can bear the consequences. If you hit a brilliant shot only to see the last few feet roll into a hazard or out of bounds, it is rather hard to swallow.

This will also come in handy as you approach some of the greens you are playing to. If you have a short iron to the green then by all means go for it. If you are standing with a 3 iron in your hand and thinking, "This probably won't make it," then drop back a club or two. It is better to be well short than catch it clean and hit it far enough to reach the lip of the front bunker. As seniors, try to apply this rule intelligently, and you will save yourself much grief. Rule number three: Lay up well short of trouble, it is a smart stroke saver.

Course management rule number four is a long one, "Experiment on the range, play on the course, and don't try anything on the course that you have not been successful with on the range." That is quite the mouthful, but it makes sense if you think about it. You are hitting your new driver like a dog on the range, but when you get to the first tee you somehow think it's now going to start working well. I don't think so! I have to giggle though, because we have all done that before. Or you stump slice one into the woods, find it, and calmly decide that a low hook 2 iron will get this ball through the hole the size of a tuna can. You have to wonder, if you were that good, what are you doing in the woods in the first place?

Anyway, if you don't hit a club well on the range, don't try it on the course until such time as you do get comfortable with it on the range.

A 60° sand wedge is another perfect example. It takes a certain feel to get that club down. Since it has more loft than any other wedge, it requires a longer swing with more velocity to go the same distance as a normal sand wedge. You need to develop that feel at practice. Otherwise, it is hard to convince yourself of how hard you need to hit it on the course to clear a bunker or the rough. You wind up dumping some shots short and putting yourself into some really bad places. Then you blame the wedge, which is only natural. The real reason is because we have not developed sufficient feel for distance with our new club.

Some well spent time on the range will overcome many of these problems, and give you a chance to experiment too. Remember rule number four: Experiment on the range, play on the course, and don't try anything on the course that you have not been successful with on the range.

How many times have you said to yourself, "If I bogey this hole, I'll shoot the lowest score of my life." You may as well have gone home then, because that inner announcement was the kiss of death. Course management rule number five is: Never add your scorecard while you are still on the course. You want to play to the best of your ability, which includes being as tension free as possible. A sure fire way to increase your tension level is to put pressure on yourself to perform as if something important depended on it. What you don't know, won't hurt you. I always know when I am playing well, I can feel it. I am also sure that if I stopped and thought about it, I would probably know my score anywhere in the round. The point is, I don't want to know because it's not going to matter until

I am done anyway. I don't want to get emotionally involved with the scorecard.

Only bad things can happen when you start adding during the round. If your score is good, the self-imposed pressure to "keep it up" starts welling inside you. If you are "stinking the place up," adding up the score can only add to your depression. If you are just playing along normally and add it up, it may force you to try to "get it going" and do something dumb. Try out rule number five next time you are playing and don't add up your score until you are done. It will help you focus on the task at hand. You should feel a new freedom without burdening yourself with the added pressure of having the outcome of your round on your mind. Ask anyone who has had the opportunity of shooting good scores and they will probably tell you they did not know where they were at until the end of the round. Keep your mind clear to make par and birdies.

Course management rule number six is: Compare yourself to no one. Now you might be thinking to yourself , "What's that got to do with course management?" but it has everything to do with playing the game well. I have a classic example of the negative effect comparing oneself to others can have on you. One of my students came to me a while back and asked if I had time for a lesson, and as we scheduled it I asked him why he wanted to get together. He, as do many students, wanted to hit the ball farther. He stated that the friends he plays with all hit the ball 300 yards (Really, I hear this all of the time) and he was sick of being outdriven by everyone he plays with.

When we got together for our lesson, he warmed up with some irons, and I asked him to hit some drivers. He actually had a beautiful swing, but was forcing it way too hard to try to get 10 extra yards out of it. He was also using an 8°, tour stiff something or other that was all wrong for his swing. It was probably the twentieth driver he had bought in the last year, searching for those extra yards. Bear in mind, he is about 70 years of age and about 5' 4" tall, and in great physical shape, so strength was not an issue. After working with him, we were getting his tee shots out there in the 230-yard area, which was a significant improvement. Off he went, happy as can be, and I had a good feeling of accomplishment knowing that I had helped him.

About three weeks later, I met up with him again, and he was on the range thrashing some new 50-inch crusher driving thing and hitting it worse than ever. I asked him what had happened? He said that his friends were still outdriving him. That is when he introduced me to his friends. Both were in their mid-twenties and looked like those professional wrestlers you see on television, built like rocks. Things became clearer very quickly.

I asked these two young chaps to hit a few, and sure enough, the one out of five that they hit went a mile, at least 280 yards. I gave them a few tips, which they were very thankful for, and called my student aside. I told him he should be able to beat these guys and he replied, "I beat them all the time, I just want to hit it as far as they do." Then it became clear to me. This poor guy spends his days in a state of frustration trying to be something he can't. He could be a great player, but is instead obsessed with distance. Golf is no fun for him because no matter how hard he tries, he can't hit it as far as the guys he is comparing himself with. The last time I saw him, he was spraying some new bulletproof mail order driver all over the place. The moral of this story is rule number six: Compare yourself to no one. Be happy with who you are, and do the best with what you have.

Course management rule number seven is, "Play to the strong part of your game." This is a pretty simple concept, yet many players don't know what their strong suits are. Do you hit it straight? Do you hit it long? Are you a good fairway wood player? What about your short game, how's that? I'll give you a few examples. I feel I have a sound all-around game and my scores reflect that feeling. However, if you were to ask me what the best part of my game is, I would without hesitation tell you it's my long iron play. Since that is my strong suit and I feel very confident with them, I will often play 1 or 2 iron off the tee and hit it as far as everyone else hits their driver. Most of the time with tremendous accuracy.

Two of the friends I often play with have their own specialties. My one friend Gary is without a doubt the best, most confident bunker player I have ever seen. He is so confident out of the bunker, that he is not afraid of a long shot to a green. I have even seen him intentionally aim for the bunker, then get up and down. My other frequent playing partner Kenny is one of the best putters I have ever seen. He hits it anywhere near the green and he is good for par or bogey at worst.

Both of these guys hit it about as far as I, but they play to their strengths and are always nipping at my heels. Dad, who doesn't hit it as far, hits it real straight, has a great short game, and is not too far off of us. He manages his game well, doesn't make many mistakes, and with the meager amount of strokes we generously give him, he is always a threat to win. We all play to our strong suits.

What is your strong suit? I ask new students this question. I say "What do you feel you do well, and what do you need work on?" Ask yourself that question. When you get the answer, be proud of what you do well, play to it, and practice the other things too. If you are a particularly good putter, then focus on getting on the green any way you can. Don't try to play to someone else's strength by trying to rip your driver a mile off the tee. To be able to use your putting, you need to be on the green. If you putt that well, then you can afford to take an extra shot getting to the green by playing safely and avoiding penalties. Know your tendencies and strong suits and play to them. No matter what it is, hitting it long, accuracy, a great short game, or anything else, try to take advantage of what you do best.

Course management rule number eight is probably more important than all of the others if we are going to lower our scores. It is, "Always be confident with your club selection." This is something we professionals do so well. If we miss a little left or right we don't mind, as long as we picked the correct club. If we hit it way long or short, then our calculation was off. Do that enough times, and your confidence starts to dwindle quickly. How many times does that happen to you? Either you make a great swing at it only to find out that you had the wrong club in your hand, or you are not sure about your club selection and make a halfhearted effort to hit it. Either usually results in a less than desirable outcome.

It is true that we have caddies to help us with the distance measurements on the course, but that's in tournaments. We still have to figure it out just like you do during social rounds, and no matter how well we hit it, if we have the wrong club in our hands it won't work.

So how can you ensure that you have the right club in your hand? It's actually much easier than most people think. First of all, we need to know how far we hit each club. How can we find that out? Either at a range or an open field, somewhere that you can hit balls and check the average distance of each club. Here's what you can do. Before you go to do this test, measure off your step on a

Figure 9.3. Learn to step off a yard with one pace.

yard stick. Since the measurements we do on the course are in yards, we need to be able to step off a yard with one pace (Figure 9.3). Take a 5, 7, 9 iron and a 3 or 5 wood to a field somewhere. Try to go on a day that it is not too windy. Start with a 9 iron after you have warmed up and hit 10 balls (the kind of ball that you play with). Pace off the distance into the center of the area the balls landed counting one step as a yard. You should know how long one of your steps is. My step is almost exactly one yard, so it's easy for me to pace something off. The amount of paces to the center of where the balls lay is the average distance you hit that particular club. In other words, if you are pacing off 9 iron shots and the first one you come to is at 65 paces and the last is 85 paces, then you hit it an average of 75 yards. Don't count any shots that were not hit decently. Do this with each club and mark it down somewhere on a file card or notebook. I feel that if we are to be confident with our club selection, we must be confident that we know how far we hit our clubs. Here is the yardage I hit mine with a full swing and no wind;

    60° wedge - 85 yards

    55° wedge - 100 yards

    Pitching wedge - 118 yards

9 iron - 130 yards

8 iron - 143 yards

7 iron - 155 yards

6 iron - 167 yards

5 iron - 181 yards

4 iron - 193 yards

3 iron - 205 yards

2 iron - 218 yards ground, 230 tee

1 iron - 235 yards ground, 250 tee

Driver - 250 - 300 yards

Notice that every gap between the clubs is not the same. I know that I have accomplished one of the major keys to accuracy by knowing how far each of my clubs will hit the ball if I put a good swing on it. I don't get any surprises on the golf course. The other benefit of knowing how far you hit each club is the pressure it takes off you. If I have a 165-yard shot, I know that if I hit a good routine 6 iron it will be the right club. Nothing fancy, no extra thoughts like, "I really have to nail this one to get it there." No, I just know that I have the right tool for the right job and use my regular swing, without forcing it. The next question is usually, "How did you know that you have a 165-yard shot?" Do we guess? Do we use the 150-yard markers? Let's find out.

THE D.W.I.T. METHOD

Many seniors I teach never learned a good way to figure out yardage correctly when playing a shot. As a result, many a beautiful swing has gone to waste by the player having the wrong club in his hands. A few years back, dad and I were discussing this and decided to figure out a simple way for a player to accurately assess their yardage, taking all the different variables into consideration. Shortly thereafter the D.W.I.T. method was born. It stands for:

D-distance

W-wind

I-incline

T-trouble

Since learning and using this method, countless students have hit more greens, including dad. He soon realized that some of the suspect results he had experienced in the past were not all bad swings, but often the wrong club selection. You will do this as part of your preshot routine, and hopefully the results will be dramatic for you too. This is one of the places the game is really played, in doing the calculations precise enough to know with confidence that you have the right club in your hand. We need to raise our level of precision higher than, "Looks like about a 5 iron to me," and D.W.I.T. will get us there. You will hit more good shots and actually play faster, so don't worry about taking a few seconds to figure out the club you need.

If you are like most people, you don't want to do a preshot routine because you are concerned about taking too much time hitting your shot. The problem is then you rush the shot, swing without being prepared, and hit many more bad shots, thereby taking longer than the golfer who set up correctly and hit it well. What is the answer? Get to your ball quickly so you have time to do your preshot routine. Slow play occurs when players are slow getting to their balls, for whatever reason. I go straight to my ball so I have time to play the game and think it through carefully.

Now let's get back to D.W.I.T after that brief but important outburst on slow play. In Figure 9.4 I am sitting near the 150-yard

Figure 9.4. I am 153 yards from the green.

marker, so I should use my 7 iron, right? Not so fast. This is a common mistake that I see when I play with students, so let's use the D.W.I.T. method and see what we really need to use. First it's the D for distance. In pacing it off, I am 153 yards from the center of the green. By the way, all yardage markers are measured to the center of the green, unless you are at some odd club that does it some other way, in which case I hope they warn you. So I am 153 to the center of the green, but the pin is in the back of the green, which makes my distance 163 yards. As a general rule, you can add or subtract around 10 yards for the different pin positions, front, center, or back. With this pin in the back, it has turned my 153 yards into 163 yards so far. W stands for wind. I play that each mile per hour of wind adds a yard. I have a five mph breeze in my face, so it now makes this shot 163 +5 = 168-yard shot. I is for incline, and as you can see, this green is elevated. Add a yard for each foot the green is elevated, and this one is about 10 feet high. That adds 10 yards to my calculation, so now I'm at 168+10 = 178-yard shot. Last is trouble, that is what the T in D.W.I.T. stands for. Notice that there is water in front of this green. If I miss, I don't want to be short. I could not get into trouble if I add a few yards to this shot.

All told, I have a shot of 180 yards to reach this pin, but I am standing next to the 150-yard marker. According to all my calculations, if I hit a 5 iron I'll be just perfect. Can you see how important it is to get good at this? Now we are playing, outsmarting the course, and using all of our senses. We are not just blindly standing there saying, "Looks like about a 7 iron." Think about it. How many of us would have played the 150-yard shot and come up miserably short? Let's go through that again only faster. Here is how I would talk to myself to figure the yardage out.

D- Distance 153, pin back 163

W- Wind at me 5, 168

I- incline (elevated) up plus 10 = 178

T - trouble short add 2 = 180 = 5 iron.

It is one of those things that you need to practice, but once you get quick at it, you will never again wonder if you have the correct club in your hand. Many seniors that I teach learned to play when distance markers were not used to the extent that they are today. I think they only can help you understand your goal more clearly. Use whatever distance markers you can find on the course. Here are some of the ones that you will see. If you look on the ground in Figure 9.4, there is a white disc marker that some courses use. A stripe of the same color is painted on the cart path to give you even more visual input. Red is normally 100 yards from the center of the green, white is 150 yards from the center, and blue is 200 yards from the center. Some even have yellow discs 250 yards from the center of the green, as if we are going to use them.

Figure 9.5 is a laser tag for measurement attached to a sprinkler head. This one tells me that it's 59 yards to the center of the green.

Figure 9.5. A laser tag.

These are neat because there are sprinkler heads all over the place and they are easy to find. Some courses use a simple system of a bush on the side of the fairway to indicate 150 yards from the center of the green. All or any of these indicators are helpful. I like being able to get fast information to help speed up play. A few courses have begun to use onboard computers that tell you on a little screen mounted on the cart your distance to the flag.

I am pretty much a traditionalist, but they were loads of fun and very interesting to use. After a few holes, I found myself getting spoiled and not thinking as much as I usually do to figure out my shot. I don't know why, but I felt like I was doing something wrong having a machine tell me within a foot the exact distance I had left. They are quite the gadgets, so if you get the chance to try one, by all means do. If you have them at your club, don't let me deter you from using them. If it helps move play along, I'm all for it. I myself find the shot much more rewarding when I figure out the yardage using my own brain. Of course, the same could be said of yardage discs and sprinkler head markers, I guess. If you don't know what measuring devices they use at the course you are playing, ask in the golf shop and they will tell you. Then you can use the D.W.I.T method and really start zoning in on the hole. Let's look at a few more examples and figure out the correct yardage.

Did you ever play a short par 4 that seemed so easy, but still chewed you up? Often what they lack in length, they make up in treachery. When you see a hole that is a par 4 and around 300 yards in length from the back tees, you know that there is a surprise somewhere. Normally, the closer you get to the green, the more dangerous it is. Here is how I would think an imaginary hole like this out. Since I need to be on in two if I am going to make a birdie, I need to leave myself a relatively easy second shot. There may be out of bounds and trees to the left, near the green I can see there is a bunker field, and water on the right near the green. Standing on the tee box, I can also see that the green is very small, which means I will need a high shot coming in to hold the green. I could rip a driver, but the chances of it working perfectly are too small and not a risk I am willing to take. Since my pitching wedge goes 120 yards, and that is what I want to leave into the green, I am going to keep that in mind as I do my D.W.I.T. Here is how I would figure out my tee shot.

D-distance -300 total length - 120 left over for second shot = 180 yards

W-wind - slight tail wind 180 - 5 yards = 175 yards

I- incline - tee is elevated, works in reverse 175 yards - 5 yards = 170 yards

T- trouble - long is the only trouble 170 - 5 = 165 yards

What started as a hole that some would be tempted to hit driver on actually calls for a 165-yard shot to play the hole the way it was designed to be played. I have always applauded golf course designers for the map they give us to play with. What map? To play a hole correctly, you need to hit it where you can see the landing area. It is true that you have a blind tee shot on occasion, but most of the time the landing area is clearly defined. It is up to us to follow the map and hit it into the target area. This last hole is a good example. How many double bogeys do you think are carded here by golfers who say "If I crush this tee shot, I'll only have a little pitch left and almost surely make birdie." Then they card a seven and this little hole claims another victim. D.W.I.T will help you get it right. Let's look at one last example:

Here is a short par 3. It is 140 yards on the scorecard. Here is how we figure it out:

D - distance: 7 paces toward the green from 140 block. 140 - 7 = 133 yards. Pin is in the middle so no added yardage for that.

W - wind: none =133 yards

I - incline: elevated green + 10 is 133 + 10 = 143 yards

T - trouble: is short add 5 yards. 143 + 5 yards = 148 yards.

So for us to have our best chance for hitting a safe shot where we will have a putt and be away from the trouble, we need to hit it 148 yards. As you get faster at it, you will be able to even assimilate more input, things like where you want to leave yourself to putt. This D.W.I.T method will give you a great handle on the shot you need to hit, then you have to pick your club and go. If you are in between clubs, you need to make the choice of which one to hit. I can tell you this from experience. You are better off gripping slightly down (½") on the longer of the clubs rather than hammering the shorter one. Swinging hard never works unless you are killing snakes.

Review all of these course management rules on occasion and be nice to yourself on the golf course. When you start to get to this level, you really get into the game. You are thinking about playing more and less about only hitting the ball, a very exciting time indeed.

The W in D.W.I.T. stands for wind. Wind is an equal opportunity annoyance that is worth touching on for a moment. There are some basic principles and rules that you should know when you are playing in the wind (15 MPH and up). When it is windy, it affects everyone equally, so be patient. If you are hitting into the wind, think trajectory not distance. In other words, if you have 100 yards left to the green, and you normally hit a high 9 iron which would get blown around by the wind, hit a punch 5 iron instead. Have your short game in good shape for those missed greens. Be creative, and expect the wind to add a few strokes to your game. Most of all, try not to let the wind frustrate you. Play it smart.

We know that time limits and finances don't always allow us a trip to the range, so here are some tips on practicing effectively at home. There are a ton of things that you can do to help your golf game, so let's go over some. Obviously, if you have a big yard or field near your home, hitting balls will certainly rate first, not to mention it's fun. When Debbie and I first got married, we lived across from the high school. I can't tell you how many balls I hit over there, but that was a special time I always looked forward to. Obviously safety must be your first concern. I would not hit real balls unless you have ample space where nothing or no one can get hit if you happen to miss hit a shot. On the course or at the range people are expecting golf balls to be hit. They know how to respond if they hear someone yell fore, which is to duck and cover your head. When someone is walking their dog, they are not expecting a golf ball to come their way. Please practice responsibly!

Putting inside on the carpet is fun too. Every time you putt a ball, you are one putt more experienced than the time before. If you have a high ceiling in the basement or garage, some big old blankets make a fine net to hit into. They also sell real netting for that sort of thing.

Plastic practice (whiffle) balls are the next best thing to real balls, as are the short-flight sponge balls. These are good for chipping and pitching around the yard without breaking anything. If you have a high level of control, a chipping net and real balls in the yard may work. Remember to be careful, as I cannot be held responsible for anything irresponsible that you do. (I'll check with my attorney, but I think that is an official disclaimer). Have a club near your favorite chair and grip the club when a commercial comes on. All of these things can help you prepare to play your best when you hit the course.

EMERGENCY CORRECTIONS ON THE COURSE

If we are doing our D.W.I.T to figure out what shot to hit, and a good preshot routine to get ourselves into position to hit it well, the only thing left is to pull the trigger and watch what happens. But what happens if you hit a bad shot? Then another? We need to learn some basics for self-correction on the golf course. I heard something long ago that made a lot of sense. It stated that the difference between a beginner, a mid handicapper, and a professional was this. All will make a mistake in their swing occasionally. The beginner will make that mistake for the rest of the round without figuring it out. The mid handicapper will make the same mistake for a few holes, then figure it out. The professional will correct it on the next swing. I know there is some truth to that, but I think all golfers can self-correct more effectively if they know what to look for. We will go over ball flight and be able to make small adjustments a bit later in this chapter, but let's look at the big one first, topping.

Is there any shot in golf that leaves you more disgusted than a top? I don't think so. A top is caused by hitting the ball on the upper half of the ball, which imparts top spin and drives the ball into the dirt. You get robbed of the one great delight in golf, watching the ball sail through the air toward its destination. In studying this for years, I have a theory on what the causes are. 1) Changing your level or spine angle on the back swing, 2) Looking away too soon, and 3) Looking at the wrong place on the ball. We will take these one at a time. If we stop one shot from being topped, it was worth it.

1) Changing your level on the back swing is a popular way to top a shot. It means that you come back to the ball at a different level than you started and hit it north of the ball's equator, thereby imparting the top spin necessary to ensure a grounder. It also makes the timing of the golf swing twice as hard. Think about it. If I stay perfectly level, my swing is timed 1-back 2 through. If you are raising up on the back swing and then trying to come back down to that same height on the way down, your timing is 1-back 2-up 3-down 4 through. Add a little sway and you have the cha-cha. Needless to say, raising up can throw a wrench into your swing. Changing your level can occur a few different ways, and here is what to look for.

A) Overswinging on the back swing can pull you out of your spine angle, which is the original angle that your spine was in at address.

B) Starting too low at address. If you start too low, when you swing back your body senses the stress on your lower back and makes you stand up to protect itself, once again lifting you out of your original spine angle.

C) Not rotating your wrists and the club correctly. If the wrists don't hinge correctly, it will yank you up every time you swing back. Once again, your body is protecting itself from wrist strain. If the club is not in a toe up position at three o'clock, your wrists are not going to hinge. If you stay on this path, up you go. This one's in chapter four also.

Check yourself against these causes and see if any of those are what is responsible for your level change in the back swing. If they occur, go back to the back swing section in chapter four to get straightened out and get rid of the level change in your back swing. If you are out on the course and need an emergency level change check up, here is a great drill to do. With the sun at your back, line up the shadow of your head with something on the ground, a leaf, a stone, or a piece of grass. Go into your back swing and watch the shadow of your head to see how much movement is in it. If it's moving around, practice a few swings until your shadow stays steady. It's a great drill except when the sun is not out.

The next probable cause of topping is simply looking at the wrong place on the ball. Golf is played on grass and there is a slight cushion under the ball. Everyone looks at a different place, but if you look at the top of the ball, sometimes you can hit the top. It will prove to you that you can hit what you look at, but result in a lousy shot. Next time you look at the ball, either look at the back bottom, or look right through the ball to the ground. It depends how much imagination you have. If you have good imagination, visualize looking through the ball and seeing the grass or tee below it. If I sound crazy to you right now, then imagination may not be your strong suit. In that case, look at the back inside quarter of the ball (Figure

Figure 9.6. Look at the back inside quarter of the ball.

9.6). Another good thought is to make believe the ball is the Earth, and you want to hit the south pole. No offense, but if you hit Canada, the shot is going into the dirt. This will help you focus on a part of the ball that will get you some results if you hit it.

The third most famous way to top the ball is to look away a little early. We just need to remember that golf is played down in front of us. That is what makes it so hard, I think. It is one of the few sports that you are not looking at the target or the field of play. If we play catch, we see each other. If we are playing basketball, we are looking at the hoop. In darts, the board is right in front of us. Not in golf though, we are expected to be patient and focus on the ball until after it's gone. It is a split-second timing, hit, then look.

"Looking up" is by far the most overused excuse for mistakes I have ever heard. If I hear one more golfer tell her friend, "You took your eye off the ball" or "You looked up," I'm going to eat garlic and breathe on them all. It should be clear to you now that there are several ways to top a ball. If you do top them, try to figure out which of these ills befalls you, so you will be able to self-correct it on the course. Also keep your eye on the ball.

BALL FLIGHT

Remember how important a follow through is. Beside allowing you to hit farther, straighter, and without injury, it has another important function for oncourse correction. When I am finished with my swing, the follow through allows me to watch the ball's flight. I am looking for two things in my ball flight, 1) The direction it started in and 2) How it is curving through the air. These two observations will tell me the type of swing path and blade angle my club had at impact. I find most senior golfers have never had a basic ball flight clinic, so here goes.

If you think about it, there are only three different swing paths and these will determine what direction the ball will start. Outside to in (Figure 9.7) will start a ball to the left. Inside out (Figure 9.8) will start a ball to the right. Slightly inside to slightly inside (straight to straight) will start a ball straight (Figure 9.9).

I went through a short phase in my career when I was pulling the ball left on almost every swing. I went and talked to one of my friends who was a well-respected professional, and he could sense how upset I was. I thought my swing was ruined. After pulling a few shots to the left, he asked me, "Jim, where are these shots going?" I said "Left." He told me that is where the club must be swinging, and that I needed to swing the club down the line where I wanted the ball to go. Then he walked away. "Rats" I thought, "I come here to get my swing fixed, and he wants me to fix it myself."

Figure 9.7. Outside to in.

Figure 9.8. Inside to out.

Figure 9.9. Straight to straight.

I finally did get it straight and realized that he was teaching me self-correction in a very simple way. Even today, if I hit a bad shot, I can fix it quickly. Also, by watching each shot, you get feedback on what is going on in your swing, and soon you can create some feel by minute changes you make in the swing path.

In all my experience, the thing that affects swing path the most is shoulder alignment. Your shoulders should be parallel to the target line, and it's very easy for them to get off line. We need to bear in mind that the shoulders are the sight on your gun, and that your swing will try to return to your shoulder position at address. O.K., that was too easy. Obviously, the shoulders square at address will give you the best chance of going straight to straight. You can check your shoulder alignment by holding a club across your shoulders in front of you after you address a ball. Sometimes it's tricky to check yourself, so if you can, get a friend to help you.

If the direction the ball starts is determined by the swing path, then any curve the ball has in the air is determined by the angle of the blade in relation to that swing path. Guess what? There are only three different blade angles: square, open, and closed. If the blade is closed, the ball will curve to the left, a hook. If the blade is open, it will curve to the right, or slice. If the blade is square or straight, bingo, it's going straight. It's as simple as that.

The grip is what effects the blade angle more than anything else, in conjunction with how you release it. To self-correct a shot that is going high and right, my first move would be to bring the left hand over the top to the right on the grip (Figure 9.10). Then when you release your hands at impact, the blade will close more and stop the ball from going right.

This is fun stuff to fool around with at the range. I think in general golfers are fearful of experimenting with these things, think-

Figure 9.10. Bring your left hand over the top of the grip in a clockwise direction to correct a high and right ball flight.

ing that they will become confused and less consistent with their swings. In time, you will see the exact opposite is true. We definitely want consistency, but we also want to expand our knowledge and feel. When you are aware of swing path and blade angle, and as you start to understand ball flight, your club head awareness develops to the point where you can actually do different shots by making subtle changes in your swing path and blade angle. How do you think we professionals do it? It's just physics, nothing fancy. We should not be afraid to experiment, if we will learn more.

Club head awareness and self-correction go together. Let's look at a few ball flights and see how they occurred and how to change them if we need to. First one is a ball that starts straight down the middle, then slices to the right. What was the swing path? Straight to straight, so it was good. How about the blade angle? It had to be open, so on the next swing we need to close it. Now you can see how important our preshot routine is. If we do the same routine each time, it eliminates some problems like ball position and feet alignment. So on the next swing, we need to get the blade closed, but how do we do that? Bring your left hand over clockwise a little and make sure you can see two knuckles on the back of it. Also, you can think about releasing your hands (rolling them over) a little more at impact. Again, try some of this stuff at the range so you don't get too many surprises on the golf course.

Our next shot starts right,and stays right with no curve. What does that tell us? It's an inside to outside swing with a square blade. I would correct by taking the club straight back and trying to swing the club what feels like more to the left. Simple as that.

Now suppose you want to control your own ball flight? Everything else being equal, make subtle changes in your swing path and blade angle. If I want to hit a high cut into a green, I take it ever so slightly outside on the take away, with a grip that is turned counterclockwise a hair. The slightly outside take away will start the ball to the left and bring the club in at a steeper angle of decent. The slightly weak (counterclockwise) grip will open the blade and give me a tiny bit of slice spin. My preshot routine is what got me aligned correctly, so I don't make all kinds of changes in how I set up. I simply translate the concept of what I am trying to do from my brain to the feel in my hands. If I want to hit a low draw (slight hook), I bring my grip into a strong (clockwise) position, take the club away inside a little, and try to release the club a little strong at impact. The inside path will start the ball on a low trajectory to the right of the target. The strong grip (see most of the back of the left hand) will close the blade at impact, and in conjunction with releasing the club, will create hook spin.

You need to try these shots when you practice. Remember a few things. Small changes have huge results. To develop good club head feel and touch, any changes that you make should be made in the smallest increments possible so that you can smoothly get accustomed to them. If you change too much too fast, it will feel uncomfortable and awkward. This may cause you to abandon a good thing too early. It usually takes about two weeks to get a feel for something new in your swing. Your success will have a lot to do with your determination. I know for a fact that anyone can get better. If you want to get better, learn more and practice what you learn.

A final note from the self-correction department. Whenever your swing seems to be leaving you on the course, slow your tempo down. We need to understand that as soon as we start hitting it poorly, our body and mind react by saying, "I'm hitting it sideways anyway, so I might as well whale it." Trust me on this one, swinging hard can only dismantle whatever control and dignity you have left. This is especially important to senior golfers, who would really like to get those extra few yards out of each shot. The little grunt at the end of each swing will only backfire. I spend plenty of time slowing students down, and it always pays off.

And yes, I am living proof that even the speediest of golfers can slow down. I am always complimented on my tempo, however anyone who knows me will attest to the fact that I am the nearest thing on earth to the perpetual motion machine. Slow down and smooth it out. I think many golfers associate golf with baseball. Yes, the swing motions are similar and the balance is the same, but there is one huge difference. In baseball, the ball is moving toward you at a very high rate of speed. We need to swing at sufficient velocity to not only counteract that speed, but to then move it in the opposite direction. That takes a heck of a lot of power. In golf, the ball is sitting motionless on the ground. We don't need to knock the cover off of it, we only need contact with smooth, accelerating velocity. Again, it's more like ballet than hockey.

THE MENTAL GAME

Let's talk about the mental side of the game a bit. As senior golfers or nearly senior golfers, we need to keep a good mental attitude about the game and what we are doing. So often senior students of mine lament the fact that they can't hit the ball as far as they used to. I think if you keep telling yourself that long enough, you will start to believe it. What we need to do is to adjust our attitude like the senior tour players do. Here are players that at one time would bring a 7,200 yard course to its knees, and now would probably have a hard time on it. Do they look like they care? Do they look like they are not having fun? They are having more fun now than when they played the regular tour, because they have made the proper mental adjustments, as well as the physical ones. We know the physical adjustments to make. Use good fundamentals, play courses that suit your length, handicap your scorecard, increase your flexibility, better course management, D.W.I.T., a better short game, and equipment that can help you play to the best of your ability. What mental adjustments can you make to help you out on the course? It once again comes down to attitude and positive thoughts.

I make sure that when I tee it up, I have no preconceived expectations of what I want to do. Sure, I have a battle plan, maybe one swing thought that I will work with during the day, but I don't think it is reasonable to tell yourself, "I'm going to shoot my best game ever today," and do it. The beauty of golf is that you never know what will happen, and so it certainly is nothing you can predict. Interestingly enough, I just came in after walking nine holes with dad, and we had a ball. I went to the course this afternoon for one thing only, to get some exercise, fresh air, and to hang out with dad, who with Mom just got down to Florida for their winter stay.

So out we went, walking and talking, just playing. Then on the ninth hole, magic strikes. It's a devilish par 5, not real long, about 480 yards. The first shot is out of a chute of trees with a very narrow landing area. I hit a particularly crisp 1 iron off the tee, as it's so dangerous that hitting a driver can only lead to disaster. I'm in the middle of the fairway with two choices. I can play it safe, hitting a 5 iron straight ahead, and then a wedge onto the green, maybe making birdie. My other option is to take it over a lake on the left, cutting around some trees, and fading it back to the green. After doing my D.W.I.T., I have about 216 yards to the flag. The point of this story is that my attitude was perfect to try this shot. How did my attitude affect my decision? I felt confident, because my attitude was upbeat and positive, as it always is. This is truly a secret that you can take with you the next time you play.

You must tell yourself that you will accept the outcome of your shots, good or bad, inquisitively, not emotionally. Remember in our ball flight that we will watch to see what direction the ball starts in and what curve it has on it? If we have a positive attitude, it works in harmony with our observations, not against them.

How often have you hit a bad shot, as we all do, or missed a very short putt, as we also all do, and dragged it with you for the rest of the round. If we have a good, positive attitude, and we simply observe the results of our shots and learn from them, we will enjoy our rounds much more. Now back to the story.

So here I am in the fairway weighing the choices, and here were my thoughts. I noticed that I had been hitting my long irons well all day, positive thought number one. It called for a fade shot, which is my favorite shot to hit with a long iron, positive thought number two. I am relaxed and playing well, positive number three.

What were the risks? The worst case scenario was to dump it in the drink, at which point a drop would leave me with a medium iron to the green. Then I made the decision to go for it. I had given myself several positive pats on the back, a good thing to do. I also knew the dangers and was willing to accept whatever outcome happened. It's important to note two things.

First, with my history of how I was hitting the ball on this day, it was not out of the realm of possibility to hit this shot. Second, if I was not hitting the ball quite as well on this particular day, I would have taken the other, more conservative route, and then congratulated myself for being so smart. I look for anything positive on every shot I take, and I think that is what makes me enjoy the game so much. I can also see it affects the players around me. I never beat myself up. If I can't find something good to say to myself, I won't comment at all. Anyway to the delight of dad, I took the shot with the 2 iron out over the lake, faded around the trees, and onto the green about 10 feet away from the pin. We were both very excited at the prospect of having a shot at an eagle, so off we went toward the green.

Dad had punched out of some trouble, but now was safely on the green. I looked at this opportunity like I look at the rest of the game, as a great blessing. There are so many who will never walk down a fairway with their friends or family, how can I possibly have a bad attitude? We got on the green, and dad putted first and drained it. I was so busy eyeing up my putt that I almost missed what a great save he made with a brilliant putt. After thanking him for showing me how it's done, it was my turn.

I had been putting well all day, so guess what? My attitude was positive again. I thought to myself, "I can see this putt" and got ready. It was a curling 10 footer, slightly downhill. The last thing I said to myself was, "It's just another putt, let feel take over." I figured that the worst I would do is make birdie, which is a great feeling in itself. But it went in, and what a way to end a day with Big Harry. I am sure we will recount that hole for a while. I will remember how a positive attitude brought about a positive result. Be nice to yourself. Think positively. If you can't find anything nice to say to yourself, then don't say anything. Feed off good shots. Let the bad ones slip away, forgotten forever.

Dad and I talked about something else on the course. He had hit a lot of good shots, then hit a bad one. He started to overcorrect himself, as he is a thinking kind of guy. After one or two more overcorrections, I suggested he play by feel. "What do you mean, feel?" he asked. I explained that he was getting far too mechanical, and looked on the verge of short circuit. I reminded him to stick to his preshot routine, trust it, and pull the trigger. He really came alive after that and I think there were a couple lessons to be learned here.

Any adjustments that you make on the course must be what I call microscopic. To produce different shots, I may change my grip slightly. Use feel on the course, that's important. I explained it to dad like this. I liken it to a data base in your brain's golf section. Each time you trust your swing and use feel, you have added a good piece of data to the feel department. If you do this enough, you develop a great feel for the game. Conversely, each time you hit a bad shot because you were too mechanical or didn't trust it, you take one piece of feel data away. So you can see how we must trust our swings, use feel, and not get too mechanical.

This all starts with the right attitude. Be positive, like yourself, and it will help you play better. Here is one final thought on attitude. As I will freely admit, even professionals don't hit it perfectly every time. It always stuns people when they see my reaction to a very bad shot. I was playing with one of my students, and was right around even par, when I flat out topped a tee shot. My student was mortified, paralyzed with fear that the great pro had actually flubbed it. That is until I turned around and, much to his relief, was smiling.

He sheepishly asked, "What happened?" to which I replied, still smiling "I missed." Simple, no excuses, no overanalyzing, I merely whiffed. I forgot it and went on, and played very well the rest of the game. When we finished, he said that watching my reaction to that shot was the highlight of his day. That is a wonderful compliment. Try to inspire others with your attitude, and set a good example of what a cool, confident golfer acts like. It can only be better for you too.

HANDLING PRESSURE

How about pressure, how can we handle that? As I have said before, pressure on the golf course is all self-imposed. We think we are under pressure, and we are if we think we are. Much of the pressure in golf comes from another preconceived notion that we should be perfect in golf. It's true, we sometimes think that every shot should be this smoothly arching draw, radar guided, honing in on its target from yards away. It's just not so. Let's put a few things in perspective.

The top professional players in the world, men, women, and seniors hit the fairway around 70% of the time. That means that three out of 10 tee shots will not be in the fairway. Those are the best players in the world. These players will also hit the green in regulation around 65% of the time. Again that means that out of

10 shots to the green, they will hit it about six or seven times. We need to keep these percentages in perspective when we tee it up. Have you been playing for a long time? Do you practice for many hours every day? Do you have an amazing amount of raw talent? If you answer no to any or all of these questions, then it's important to look at your game logically. If you want to be half as good as the best players, then you would want to hit three out of 10 fairways, and three out of 10 greens that you shoot at. Keep track of your own statistics when you are playing. Those seem like more reasonable goals than hitting every green and fairway like some golfers think they should.

To take the pressure off ourselves, therefore, we should set reasonable goals. To attain those goals, we need to be emotionally detached from our round of golf. Here is a classic example of that detachment. A few months ago, one of my assistant professionals and I went to a course to work on our games. As we were about to tee off, two of my students, a very nice couple, pulled up to the tee. When they looked up and saw us, they were delighted, until the starter said that they must play with us because a large group was coming out. Then a look of paralysis came over them. Upon seeing this, I walked over and explained something to them.

I told them that we were here to play. That's it. If they needed help with something, they were free to ask, but other than that, we were just going to play. I explained that they should seize the opportunity to watch a few professionals play up close, and learn from it. Also, I didn't care what they shot, because that is not how people should be judged. I judge people by who they are, not what they shoot, and I think very highly of them both.

With that little speech, we went out to play. Not only did we enjoy a wonderful day together, but they both played the games of their lives, with our lady friend making two birdies on the same holes as I. They are still talking about that round. I think the fact that they overcame what could have been a very high-pressure situation is what made it so special.

This is what you must do when you go out. Give yourself a little pep talk. Realize that it really doesn't matter what you shoot, it matters who you are. If you are relaxed and not trying too hard, you will be able to do your best. How do we know that is true. Simple. Think back to a round that you were really bearing down, trying as hard as you could, and hitting it poorly. At some point, you figured the round was ruined by your terrible play, so you quit focusing and just hit it. You didn't care about a thing. What happened? After you "gave up" and took the pressure off of yourself, you started playing wonderfully.

I did this in a practice round for a tournament very early in my career. I was playing with some very good professionals and boy, did I want to do well. After embarrassing myself with a 46 on the front, I gave up and didn't try as hard. What I really did was take the self-imposed pressure off of myself and shot 33 on the back nine? Go figure. So do your D.W.I.T., a good preshot routine, observe your shot, and remain emotionless to bad shots. Don't pressure yourself into performing well. Be nice to yourself and take the pressure away.

I am a firm believer that you can help the outcome of your game by what you do when you arrive at the course to play. I drive my friends crazy because I don't want to get there an hour early and hit five jumbo baskets at the range. I find that the longer I hang around before I tee off, the more things I can find wrong with my swing. I only like to hit a few balls, if any, before I tee off. To me, it is much more important to stretch completely (chapter two), and putt as many as you like to get a good stroke. That is a routine that builds confidence.

If you start beating balls, sometimes since you are excited about playing, you start to get fast. Then something can creep into your swing, and the next thing you know, you are a basket case with no confidence heading to the first tee. I figure that if I didn't know it when I got to the course, I'm not going to learn it on the range. You know yourself better than I, so do what is right for you. Use the range before teeing off as warm-up only, and keep your warm up hitting short and sweet. Go putting, which will pay itself back on the course.

FIXING A BROKEN SWING

Suppose that you have something going haywire in your swing, how should you approach fixing it? A good plan is to check the basic functions of the swing, grip, aim, and set up first. If you can identify the problem, go to the range and work on it. If everything looks good, give yourself a rest, maybe a day or two, and try again.

You may have been tired or stressed out. If after a while you are still hitting it poorly, you may want to go take a lesson. Golf instruction, as you can tell by what is in this book, has come miles in the last 10 years. So many new discoveries and methods make learning much easier than it was before, many of my new senior students have never taken a lesson before, and are absolutely stunned by how much better they get in a short amount of time. There are private lessons and clinics, but the first thing you need is a good, respectful, helpful instructor.

Here are a few guidelines to help you get one. Find a P.G.A. or L.P.G.A. teaching professional who comes highly recommended by someone you know. Talk to that professional about the problem that you are having. Ask him or her about themselves too. You were not born yesterday, so you should be a good judge of character. If you do not like them as a person, you will not like them as an instructor.

Sign up for only one lesson. Anyone who says it will take x amount of lessons to fix your problem can't be very confident in his ability. Here is how I figure it. I can correct any problem someone has in one lesson. He leaves with a clear understanding of the root of the trouble he has been having and a drill to correct it. If he practices the drill, he will conquer the problem, simple.

The reason so many of my students return to see me is after they correct the initial problem they were having, they want to learn more and get even better. That is the greatest compliment I could ask for, a satisfied student. If you take a lesson from someone, and after practicing what they recommend you don't get any results, you shouldn't go back. Also, it's not a good idea to have a friend's friend help you because he is a "pretty good golfer."

That means nothing when it comes to instruction. Leave it to the professionals. When you find a good professional who helps you, work on what he says intensely. In golf, you will only get out what you put in. I guess that goes for life too. So whether it's private or clinic lessons, it's the instructor who makes it good or bad.

If you decide to go to a clinic or group lesson, make sure that the student-teacher ratio is no more than one instructor for each eight students. The reason you go to a group or clinic lesson is to share the expense with the other students, which is fine. If there are 60 people there, chances are you will not get any personal attention. If you are in a clinic with around six or seven other students, and have a good instructor, it's a way to get more than your money's worth. Ask lots of questions.

500

Same thing goes with private lessons. I have studied the game of golf deeply for years and nothing makes me feel better than to share that knowledge with my students. When I am teaching, I enjoy answering questions that students want to ask a professional. That is what I have worked so long for. Ask lots of questions and you will not only learn more, you'll make the professional earn his pay. Remember that there is no such thing as a stupid question. The only stupid question is the one you don't ask. The reason we know the answer is because we have already asked it at one point in our careers.

Where else can we learn more? There are books, videos, magazines, and all sorts of information out there. You will read and hear many tips from as many different sources. Keep a few things in mind. First of all, there is such a thing as sensory overload, which is learning so much that you can't think straight any more. If you are becoming paralyzed with too many thoughts, stop learning and return to basic fundamentals immediately; grip, aim, and posture. Secondly, all instructors are different. You should try anything that you think will help your swing at least once. If it feels good, continue with it. If after serious practice it still feels terrible and you don't see any results, try something else. Watch some golf on television. Watching the professionals will teach you how to play yourself out of bad situations, and you can learn from watching their tempo. I would be careful how much instruction you get from the tube. You may short circuit your brain with too much information.

SAVING A FEW BUCKS

Since we are not all millionaires, I figured I would share with you some financial tips in the golf industry, ways you can save some money if you either want to or need to. This becomes ever more important as more golfers have fixed incomes or retire and have to watch their spending. If you buy a glove, get either an all-leather or synthetic with leather on the palm and fingers. The all-synthetic gloves don't breathe very well.They can get hot and sticky. In the summer, if it's hot where you live, get two gloves to play with and rotate them. Play one hole with one glove, and then hang it on your cart or bag to dry and wear the other glove for the next hole. This will prevent them both from getting too wet and wearing out prematurely.

As your gloves get beat, use them for practice and save the good ones for playing. Never put a glove all scrunched up in your bag pocket unless you want it to feel like a potato chip when you pull it back out. Either hang it on the outside of your bag or hang it on a club when you get done playing. It must air dry to retain its softness. Just by gripping the club correctly you will save money on gloves.

Golf balls are all personal preference; however, there are some bargains to be found. Golfers are funny about balls, so if you have a favorite and will not switch, I understand. For all the rest of you golfers, listen up and start saving. Don't buy golf balls at the course unless you know they have good prices. I always snoop around at the clubs and check prices. Some are fair, but at some places you need to take out a loan for a sleeve of balls. You can buy the multiple-ball packs that sell 15 and 18 balls for the price of 12. You can buy slightly experienced balls (fished from ponds by divers) for about ½ of the price of new balls. If you can find x-outs, there is a real money saver. They go for the ½ the price of the same ball brand new. So what's an x-out? It is a ball that has failed the last inspection at the golf ball factory. It was one tiny blemish or a misprint away from being a grade A, brand new ball. As I was getting better, I used them for practice and never noticed any difference. Be warned that they are not approved for tournament play, because they have not gone through the final inspection and approval. Don't tee up an x-out at the city championship. All the rest of the year, save some bucks. We know that custom built clubs are actually less expensive than the big name (big advertised) clubs.

Clothing outlet stores have some sharp shirts and slacks at a fraction of the cost of department stores. You are going to get them loaded with sunscreen and perspiration anyway, so unless you can afford it, forget the $50.00 shirts. You can get hats at those stores, too. By the way, did you know that you can wash your hats and visors in the dishwasher? There are wire racks that you can buy that hold the hat rigid as the dishwasher does its thing. You won't believe how clean it can get a hat that you were sure things were growing on.

How about the course? Please remember that I am telling you these things so that you are aware of them. Some could care less, but to some golfers saving a few bucks can mean the difference between playing and staying home. I would rather see you out playing. First, walk when you can. You will save a ton on cart fees and it's better for you anyway. If you are healthy, you will also play better walking. You can get into the flow of the game, ponder life as you walk along, and generally stop and smell the roses. Take advantage of the twilight rates, it usually changes at around two o'clock. With the late sunset in the summer, you can generally play 18 holes at a greatly reduced rate. Drink water instead of buying a $2.00 soda. Put a snack in your bag from home. Again, this is not for everybody, but the course will not suffer. They have plenty of people paying the full rate all day and loading up on goodies. The reason they have special rates at certain times of the day is to get golfers on the course at otherwise quiet times. Hopefully, these tips will help you save a few bucks to spend on green fees so you can play more. That is really what golf is all about.

TO SUM IT UP

This will wrap up our chapter on playing and practicing. Let's review a few key points, shall we? If we are going to experiment, which we should, the range is the place to do it. After we have settled in on a swing, we want to make our practice as lifelike as possible, not just hit balls into space with no target or purpose. We must do a preshot routine each time we hit at the range to get it down so we can transpose our swing onto the golf course. We need to dismantle a hole backwards, and we can use the D.W.I.T. method for all of our full swings.

We will develop feel and a super short game for everything inside a full sand wedge, whatever that distance may be for you. Our ability level should dictate the courses and tee boxes we play from, not our ego. Pre handicapping the score card takes pressure off us and simple self-correction is a goal we should all strive for.

Our final goal is club head awareness; to be able to hit different types of shots. We should maintain a positive, inquisitive attitude when we play or practice. It's also important that we don't expect too much or put too much pressure on ourselves. Take a lesson if you want to, and find a good professional to teach you. If you need to save a few bucks, follow the tips and get creative. Never, ever forget how blessed you are to be out on the course. Above all else, we need to remember that it can never be mastered, only enjoyed. That is why we play. The challenge, the fun, and the camaraderie. Never stop learning and you will never stop enjoying.

Additional Facts for Ladies Only

I am very excited about all of the women entering the game of golf. Women make up about 32% of all the new golfers learning the game, and, living in an area with many seniors, about 50% of my new students are senior ladies. Their presence is stronger than ever in a game that was traditionally played mostly by men. That, in my estimation, is the way it should be. We all love playing the game of golf, and golf is a game to be enjoyed by everyone. I now teach many more couples than before and I applaud that too. What a great way to get some exercise, fresh air, and spend some time with someone you enjoy being with. It is now not uncommon for women to simply go to the course and get paired with a group of golfers, whereas there was a time not long ago when this was unheard of. So times are changing for the better, and lots of ladies are joining in the fun. That is why I am writing this section. This entire book applies to both men and women, however there are important adjustments that must be taken into consideration by you lady golfers. We will discuss all of those things in this chapter, so you can play your best and have more fun.

WE ARE ALL DIFFERENT

The first and most important point that we need to address is that men and women are built differently. I have said earlier in this book that we are all individuals, and as such we need to adopt a swing that fits our bodies. Women have several major differences with their bodies than a man's body that affect the golf swing. First is the chest structure, second is their center of gravity, and the third is upper body and arm strength. If we take these differences into account, we will see that a lady's golf swing is similar, yet slightly different than a man's. Let's talk about those differences and give you a swing that fits you.

Women are generally not as strong in the upper body as men. Many women consider this a handicap, but it really isn't. Since most women don't possess massive upper body strength, they tend to swing more smoothly and hit it off line less often than men. The good news is women are much more flexible in their upper bodies, especially seniors. It is obvious then, that we must take advantage of a woman's superior flexibility without having a golf swing that relies too much on upper body strength.

Also, women have a harder time releasing the golf club with a strong wrist and forearm move like the men. This is where men can create extra distance, but it is different with women. How can we get more distance out of the ladies? We will use a stronger left hand grip, one that we can see three knuckles on the back of the left hand, thereby setting a better angle and hitting the ball more solidly at impact. How do you know which one of these swings to use? It would depend on your athletic ability, upper body strength, and sports history. If you hit a 7 iron over 110 yards, or have been involved with sports for a long time, then you can follow the first program described in this book. If you do not feel very athletic, have not been playing sports for a long time, or don't feel like you have a very strong upper body, then you will use the program described in this chapter.

A woman's center of gravity is different than a man's, it is lower to the ground. This is evidenced by the fact that many of the ladies that I teach feel they need to "sit down" at address, which is to overflex your knees and put your weight on your heels. This puts them in a very nonathletic position and makes it a struggle to contact the ball solidly, especially with the irons. When you "sit down", your swing becomes flat, which is to swing the club around your back more than up to your shoulders where it should be. Since you can get away with this flat swing more with the woods than the irons, many women favor their woods. In addition to not coming into the ball at a good angle, this sitting-down position will rob you of much of your body's power. It would be equal to you only hitting the ball with your arms. So even if you can hit your woods in a sitting-down position, you will hit them farther with a more balanced swing. Since we don't associate ladies with massive arm strength, sitting down could pose a real problem in the power department. You can combat this tendency by taking out some of the knee flex in your legs, bending at the waist more, and making sure you are on the balls of our feet. This will also greatly affect your short game and your ability to get your chips and pitches into the air.

How can we feel if we are on the balls of your feet? We know that the balance is the same for golf as it is for softball, tennis, and all other athletic sports. But what if you have not played any of these? Do you dance or ski? Both of these use the same balance, too. What happens if you go to your heels when you are skiing? You wipe out, don't you? Could you dance with your weight on your heels? I don't think so.

Look at Figures 10.1 and 10.2 pictures of our golfer. In the first picture she is sitting on her heels and is out of balance. In the second picture she is athletic and ready to swing. She is in balance and on the balls of her feet. In the first picture, she is sitting down with too much knee flex. This lowers her center of gravity, and she doesn't stand much of a chance of hitting the ball solidly. Here are a few drills to get you balanced correctly. If you have ever played softball, get your grip and put the club up on your shoulder like a bat. Get flexed as if you were going to hit a softball pitched to you (Figure 10.3). Now simply sole the club on the ground while you keep the same balance. This will put you in a good position to hit from, properly balanced and athletic. If you have not played any baseball-type sports, try this drill with dancers' feet. Set up to a ball in your normal fashion. See if you can dance your feet back and forth. If you were on your heels, you had to move your weight to the balls of your feet to "dance." That is a good drill to use to get ready to hit. Be balanced and you will be able to use your body to get more distance. Your shots will

Figure 10.1. On your heels with too much knee flex is not a very athletic position.

feel more solid and you will feel a lot more strength in your swing.

The grip that women use will be a little different than a man's grip. First of all, it must fit your hands. If you have particularly large or small hands, get your grip size checked by a profes- sional. Like everyone else, you deserve to be fitted cor- rectly, not just told to use a woman's grip.

Figure 10.2. This is a set up for success, very athletic and balanced.

Figure 10.3. Batter up! This softball set up will teach you balance.

Look at our golfer's grip in Figure 10.4. You can see three knuckles on the back of her left hand, and the club is down in the fingers of her left hand, not up in the palm. This is important for several reasons. At the be- ginning of this chapter we were discussing that a lady will not release the club with the forearm strength that a man uses. Instead, we will create a solid angle between the wrists and club on the back swing. This will also help counter-act the fact that a woman's chest is generally larger than a man's. Men can swing their arms across their chests much easier than women. By using a grip with a stronger left hand, women can make this solid angle of power on the back swing without having their arms fly away from their bodies in an effort to accommodate their chest. Holding the club in the fingers of the left hand will maximize your control. If it rides up into the palm of your left hand, all control is lost. Look at Figure 10.4. Notice the angle of the wrists. This is the angle that loads up power and maintains the power through-out the back swing and down swing. If we don't have this angle in our back swing, or we unload it early coming down to the ball, we will not realize the power we deserve in our swing. If you go into your back swing position with your left arm at nine o'clock parallel to the ground, the club should be pointing straight up with your wrists fully cocked. That is a great angle for power.

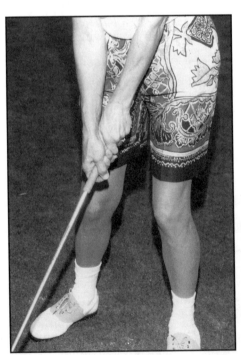

Figure 10.4. See three knuckles on your left hand.

Generally speaking, most women are much more likely to have trouble with their back swing than forward swing. Armed with her tremendous flexibility, it is easy for a woman to overswing going back. This is a problem for more than one reason. First of all, if you go too far back it is hard to get the club back on the ball squarely. This can result in many miss hits and glancing blows at impact. Secondly, you are much more likely to break down your left arm extension if you overswing, causing a loss of power and accuracy. If your left arm bends and you lose extension in your arms, it makes the swing harder to time because you have another hinge at the elbow that should not be there.

So a woman's flexibility can be a blessing if used correctly, and a hindrance if abused. How do we use this gift of flexibility appropriately? We need to know how far we can go back and still maintain extension, balance, and power. Try the five-second drill. Address a ball with the correct grip (where you can see at least three fingers on the back of your left hand), and good extension in your left arm (Figure 10.5). Now turn in to your back swing and hold it for five seconds. We are looking for the same criteria as in chapter three on the five-second drill:

1) Your shoulders should not move your head more than 1" off the ball on your back swing.

2) You retain soft extension in your left arm. It should be straight, not bent, but also soft, not rigid. There should be a 90° angle between your club and left arm.

3) You should be relaxed and in balance.

4) You must be able to clearly see the ball.

When you get to the top of your back swing, check one last thing. Many ladies lift their left heel way of the ground on the back swing. This is often a result of poor set-up fundamentals or grip, and just isn't necessary. If it comes off the ground slightly, that is acceptable. You have more than enough flexibility to create power

Figure 10.5. Great set up with a solid grip and soft extension in the arms.

without lifting the left heel way off the ground. If your heel is moving that much, then your body level is changing with it, which adds another aspect of timing to your swing and makes it harder to impact the ball solidly. Work on your back swing and get a good power angle through good fundamentals.

Often I see my women students without the proper arm extension. This can lead to all kinds of mishaps on the down swing. When you are at address, make sure your arms are softly extended, but not rigid.

Those are the basic changes that a woman needs to make in her swing. Aside from those changes, all of the other theories in the previous chapters apply to your swing. Staying level, follow through, tempo, short game, etc. Adapt the changes to your swing and practice as much as you can. The better you get, the more you can enjoy playing.

HOW WOMEN PLAY WELL

Which brings us to our next point, playing. You need to know a few things as women. There are two facets of the game that I think women need to focus their attention on more than men, the short game and consistency. I play with a lot of female students, and of course, my wife. I don't expect them to hit the ball as far as I do, but that doesn't diminish the fact that I enjoy playing with them. We need to keep a few things in perspective.

First of all, the average lady's tee shot is around 130 yards, so if you hit it this far you are doing well. Here is what my years of observation have taught me. The good women players whom I have played with did not hit it much farther than that, they just hit it every time. They also possessed a fabulous short game, being able to get up and down from anywhere around the green. They were all phenomenal putters, holing putts from everywhere.

I think that the average lady feels that if she doesn't hit it as far as a man, the men will have no respect for her game. So she tries overly hard to hit it far, which results in bad shots and makes her nervous. The ladies who are good players know their limitations and play to them. I have been in mixed groups before with solid women players and men players. The men were very impressed with the ladies' consistency and short games; everyone had a ball and were equals. Let's assess more specifically what we need to do to play better.

First of all, you need a good tee shot that gets you into play. Know that distance is overrated as the only important aspect of golf. Since consistency is so much more important, your tee club should be a club that you can easily hit. A 3, 5, or 7 wood is the best bet. Drivers are good if you are a good player, and then they should be at least 13° loft. Practice this shot like crazy, so you have confidence in it, and can get off the tee in front of others. I mean really practice this shot.

Think back to how you feel when you hit it solidly off the first tee. It doesn't matter how far you hit it, but if you hit it out there solidly, you gain the instant respect of the other players. It will also build your confidence when everyone says "nice shot" as you put your club back into your bag.

Now think back to how lonely the first tee can be when you top one about 15 yards and are met by silence. Regardless of the wood you use, you will feel better if you know that you have a good chance of hitting it off the tee. Get very comfortable with it. When you practice it, make sure you do your preshot routine each and every time that you hit a practice ball.

Next, you need an advancement shot. That is a shot that advances the ball down the fairway straight and consistently. Whatever club you want to use, it should be one that you can become very consistent with. I would either use a 5 or 6 iron, or a 7 or 9 wood. It should be a club that you can hit eight out of 10 times. Remember, it doesn't have to go a mile, it just has to go. It is the same thing as our tee shot, we can't afford to give away a stroke by topping it 15 yards. We need all the distance we can muster on each advancement shot, as long as it is consistent. That shot will get us into the realm of what should be our true specialty, the short game. There is not a lady reading this who can't and shouldn't get as good as a professional at the short game. Since men have an advantage in the distance department, the ladies should have an advantage in the finesse department. If we are to be competitive and play our best, we need to be short game magicians. Learn from the short game chapter in this book and increase your ability to score. So have a game plan to 1) get off the tee and into play, 2) advance to around the green, and 3) chip or pitch it close to the hole and putt it in. Sounds like fun.

YOUR EQUIPMENT

You will notice that I have mentioned a tee shot club, an advancement club, and short game clubs. You do not need 14 clubs in your bag to play effectively. Even many of the LPGA ladies are carrying some interesting sets of clubs now, designed to fit a woman's needs. If you had your tee club, your advancement club, then 6, 7,8,9, pw, sw, and 60° wedge and putter, that would probably avoid having too many options. I would rather see you get really good with a limited amount of clubs, then have a ton of clubs in your bag and struggle with them all.

For ladies who are starting, another good set makeup is 5 wood, 4, 6, 8, pw, and putter. As women, you have been forced to accept the same set makeup as a man's set as "standard." This "standard set" doesn't take a woman's needs into account very effectively. That gives you 14 clubs in the bag and is very confusing. Many of the clubs will appear to go the same distance.

Get custom-fitted clubs that are made for you. Get the exact number of clubs that you want and no more. If you or one of your lady friends are just starting, try to buy a used woman's club at a second hand golf or sports store to begin with. What historically has happened is ladies would wind up with a cut-down man's club. A cut-down man's club is often too heavy and has too stiff a shaft for a lady to handle. Is it any wonder why so many women get discouraged and don't want to play? That's like me golfing with a sledgehammer. Even I would lose my enthusiasm under those con-

ditions. Get a set that fits you and enjoy the benefits of good, properly fitted equipment. It is amazing what ill effects poorly fitting
clubs can have on a woman's swing. You could never imagine how
often I see this on the lesson tee. Let's take the first example of a
woman's club being too short for her. This bends the golfer over too
much, which will make it very difficult for her to maintain her
spine angle going back. She will want to stand up to relieve pressure
from her back. On the way back down, she must time it perfectly or
she will hit it heavy, top it, or miss.

How about a club that is too long, is that bad too? Yes, easily
as bad as a club that is too short. The toe of the club will point up
into the air, which almost negates the sweet spot unless the ball is
on a tee or perched up in the grass. That is why I hear the common
complaint from women that they hit it well off the tee, but have
trouble off of tight fairways. Also, a club that is too long will cause
a flat swing plane that has the club swinging around the back too
much.

Plenty of misshits await the golfer whose clubs don't fit. I think
the part that saddens me is the fact that often it's actually a good
swing motion that is being held back by ill-fitting clubs. Then a
person quits from lack of interest, when they may have been a great
golfer if only they had clubs they could hit. Try different clubs and
be curious. Don't stop looking until you find exactly what you are
looking for and are sure they fit.

PICK THE RIGHT COURSES TO PLAY

Just like the men, but even more so, it is critical that women
golfers play a course that is user friendly. The front tee boxes should
be significantly shorter than the men's white tees. If they are not, try

to find a course that is fair to women. Many of the old style courses just put a set of red tees 10 feet in front of the men's tees and call them ladies tees. This is not very fair. Ladies possess about two thirds of the upper-body strength as a man of equal size. It would make sense, therefore, that the ladies tee box or markers should be about two thirds the distance of the man's tees from the green, this would make it so every golfer had a chance. If a hole was 340 yards for the men, it would play about 230 for the ladies. That would be driver, six iron for both players, men and women. I think in the future as more women come into the game, the tee markers will be more fair to ladies. I hope so. I know that I would have a hard time playing a 9,000-yard course, which is what happens proportionally when you make the women play from near the men's tees. The newer courses are heading in this direction, and that's good news. Hopefully, the courses that refuse to accommodate women will see that reflected in their lack of income, courtesy of all the ladies who go elsewhere to play.

As odd as it may sound, I always recommend that the ladies check and make sure there are adequate facilities at the course for women. This includes a place for ladies to change and restrooms on the golf course itself. I can think of nothing more uncomfortable than to be on the forth hole, needing to use the facilities, and finding out the next opportunity is an hour away. That falls under the heading of cruel and unusual punishment. If you are a member of a club, it's often as simple as letting the head professional or general manager know your suggestions and concerns. They are there to help you, and most often will do so if they are aware of what the membership needs.

DEALING WITH THE HELPERS

Golf is supposed to be fun, and it should be. Try to find respectful partners to play with. If you play with someone you do not enjoy playing with, don't play with them again. A very common scenario I come across is the male and female team golfing together. Sometimes this is a wonderful match, but it can also lead to a very stressful situation for both parties. The male is so excited about his friend golfing with him that he can hardly contain himself. He also wants to help. He wants to make sure every shot she hits is perfect, every putt goes in, every chip stops 3" from the cup, every club she selects is correct and so on. She does not even finish her swing before he, ever helpful, has a complete analysis of the ball flight, what she did wrong, what part of her swing broke down, and how she can correct it on the next swing.

From lack of knowlege, the terms "you looked up" or "keep your left arm stiff" permeate the air over and over. She becomes so paralyzed with thought that now she doesn't stand a chance in the world of getting one airborne. Finally in disgust, he politely suggests "just hit the #$$¢&¢%%** thing." She really feels great now. Sound familiar? You must remember that this is all said by the husband or friend in an effort to help and has no malicious intent. The problem is that no one can play under that kind of pressure, no matter how innocent the intentions are.

When someone is learning, they need to make mistakes and figure out things themselves. That is called learning. It always surprises everyone who plays with my wife and me, how little technical advice I give her. I want to enjoy her company, not shortcircuit her brain with a million complex thoughts. If she hits a bad shot, looks up and says, "What did I do?", I'll even sometimes answer her with a humorous but respectful, "You missed." Then she goes on her merry way without too much baggage on the brain and often corrects the problem herself. If I see a glaring problem, and see that she is becoming frustrated, I will offer a simple explanation and correction.

One of the first rules of teaching I learned in my P.G.A. education was at all costs, don't overteach. Even when I work on another professional's swing, or one works with me on mine, we keep it very simple.

I am asked this next question more often than you could ever imagine by my women students. How do we politely keep the helpers from overhelping without hurting any feelings? In my experience, the best way to handle this is to respectfully lay down some ground rules that will prevent embarrassing situations from ever arising. I liken it to when two couples go out to dinner. No matter how uncomfortable it is to request separate checks, it sure beats how bad you feel when the other couple orders the caviar-stuffed lobster and you order a pot pie.

First of all, tell them how excited you are to be playing with them, which hopefully you are. Tell them that although you know they are only trying to help, it is very difficult for you to think of too many things at once. Since you want to have fun, and you don't want this to be like work, make a deal with them. Request that they give you the opportunity to learn by watching them. They can even briefly describe the shot they are going to do for you. When it's your turn, you will hit your shot and learn from it, without comment from them. If you have a specific question, you will ask them, which you should. Hopefully this will stop the overteaching.

There are two circumstances that I play with students, one is a playing lesson, and the other is just to play. When it's a playing lesson, I discuss in advance what they want to accomplish and what they have difficulty with. When we get to the course, I simply let them play so I can observe how they handle various shots. When we get to any of the shots that they have difficulty with, we go over a better way for them to accomplish their goals. That is a playing lesson. If I am simply going out to play a round with students, I just let them play. No comments, no suggestions, only encouragement and a "nice shot" when they hit one. If someone has a question, I am more than happy to answer it for them. After the round, if asked, I will offer my suggestions on how they might improve. That is how a professional does it. If, in your case, the person you play with still insists on giving you unsolicited advice, let them read this. If worse comes to worse, you may have to tell them that if it doesn't stop, you will not play with them any more. Hopefully, the problem will never progress that far.

LEARNING THE RIGHT WAY

So what do you do if you need help with your swing and can't figure it out yourself. I always recommend seeking the help of a good P.G.A. or L.P.G.A. teaching professional. They should come recommended by someone you know or have played golf with. Not all professionals teach alike. Not all teaching professionals need to be world-class players, either. Don't pick an instructor by her playing accomplishments, rather choose one with satisfied students. Talk in person with your prospective instructor. Watch closely and you will be able to see how respectful and genuine they are. If all they do is talk about how great they play, they will probably do that during the lesson too. You are the one who has to make the call. Get references and use your gut feeling.

When you take a lesson, only sign up for one to start, unless it's an instructor whose style you know you like. After you take your first lesson, you will be able to judge better if this instructor is someone you can work with. This happens all too often in the golf business. Someone signs up in advance for six lessons and then doesn't like the way the person is teaching them. The main thing is to get a respectful, respected instructor, male or female, who will listen to your needs and help you. They should help you with sound fundamentals and be encouraging. You should always leave better and more knowledgeable than when you got there.

Group clinics are another good way for you to learn and progress. Again, make sure you know someone who has gone through one, or ask to call one of the students at random from the last class. Get with an instructor that you like as a person. Prices vary on these clinics depending on the student-teacher ratio, so try to get into a class that doesn't have more than about eight students per instructor. Then you will get some personalized attention. Clinics where there are 50 people and one instructor playing simon sez don't appear very effective to me. Wherever you go, you should meet more nice people to play golf with, and that is always fun.

TO SUM IT UP

In review, play courses that you like with people you like. Gracefully but firmly reject overteachers. Take a lesson from a good, highly recommended professional if you need help or want to learn more. Get the right clubs and set make up for you. Make the proper adjustments to allow for the differences in your body from a man's. Get a consistent tee shot, advancement shot, and brilliant short game. Then get out there and have a ball.